Changed

Karen Bishop

Copyright © 2024 by Karen Bishop

All rights reserved.

No portion of this book may be reproduced in any form without written permission from the publisher or author, except as permitted by U.S. copyright law.

Contents

1. Chapter One: Running — 1
2. Chapter Two: Doorbells Ringing — 11
3. Chapter Three: Burning Water — 19
4. Chapter Four: Breakfast — 34
5. Chapter Five: Surprise Visitor — 43
6. Chapter Six: Bubble Bath — 53
7. Chapter Seven: Doctor — 61
8. Chapter Eight: News — 75
9. Chapter Nine: Christmas — 83
10. Chapter Ten: Shopping — 92
11. Chapter Eleven: April Twenty Eighth — 104
12. Chapter Twelve: Wrestling — 127
13. Chapter Thirteen: Sexist — 141
14. Chapter Fourteen: Family Lawyer — 148
15. Chapter Fifteen: 11:52PM — 165

16. Chapter Sixteen: Hose   183

17. Chapter Seventeen: Incompetence   197

18. Chapter Eighteen: It Won't Be Like This For Long   217

Chapter One: Running

Chapter One: Running

"Just yank it!" I say frantically to my husband. I feel him tugging at the zipper.

"Baby, it won't go."

"No, no no no, that's impossible. It fit perfect two weeks ago!"

"The zipper is probably broken." He says calmly.

"Fuck it! I'm not going."

"Sweetheart, you have to go." He says gently.

"Get me out of this dress please. Please unzip it."

I feel the zipper doing down and I slip out of the dress, marching out of the bedroom in my panties.

"Sweetheart, you're Megan's maid of honor and I'm Justin's best man. You have to go." Danny says gently.

"How? I can't get into the damn dress."

"Let's just try one more time." He says gently. "I think the zipper is broken."

I cover my breasts with my hands and stare out the window at the water.

I feel his hands on my arms and his lips press softly on my cheek.

"Come on sweetheart, let's try one more time."

I know I have to go to that wedding, so I take a deep breath and walk back into the bathroom, my heels clicking on the floor.

"By the way," Danny says following me. "We should have sex sometimes with your heels on. I kind of dig it."

"We can have sex right now. Let's just stay home."

"Megan needs you." He says. "We can have all the sex you want tonight."

I sigh.

"Fine."

He helps me get the dress on. It slides easily over my hips.

"This time, squish them down." He says.

I get the fabric over my breasts and press on them, wincing.

Yeah, I'm definitely going to start my period soon.

He tugs on the zipper a little bit and then it slides right up.

"See?" He says. "You're in!"

I look in the mirror to make sure my makeup is on point, and then I turn to my husband. He's wearing the tuxedo and the purple bow tie and I'm wearing the purple dress that matches his bow tie.

I reach up to fix his hair and then walk into the bedroom, grabbing m clutch purse off of my bed.

"When we get home, we're having a gym installed downstairs."

"You don't need a gym." He sighs. "You're incredibly beautiful."

"In a week I'm going to be fat. You watch."

I march down the stairs, my heels clicking on the wood floors. I walk into the kitchen and pour Pepper's bowl of dog food so it's full.

Danny follows me down to the basement and I walk into the garage, turning to him.

"Let's take your car." He says.

"Fine, but I'm driving." I take the keys to my Jeep from his hand and unlock it.

Upon getting inside, I hit the button to open the garage door. Danny gets into the car too and I back out.

Megan is getting married here in Wilmington at the same park Danny and I got engaged at. If you look across the water from our backyard, you can see the park.

Since our house is large, most of Danny's family is staying at over house tonight.

I don't mind. I'm obsessed with our house and I'm very cocky about it.

I know our house is amazing. Who wouldn't want to stay in it?

I shut the garage door with the button and pull out onto the street.

I drive to the exit of our neighborhood and turn right.

I cross over the bridge to the canal and take the first right.

I follow the path to the parking lot and stop the car. Work cars are everywhere bringing supplies and decorations.

"If my zipper busts, we run, okay?"

"Yeah." Danny gets out and I follow him.

We stop in the hall and one door says bride and the other says groom.

"I'll see you in a few hours." Danny kisses my lips.

"Okay, love you."

"Love you." He replies. He disappears behind the groom door and I slip into the bride room.

Everyone is already here.

"Am I late?" I ask.

"No." Megan shakes her head, sitting down on the couch with a bowl of cereal. "Why are you already ready? The wedding isn't for like, three hours?"

"How are you so calm?" I ask her.

She shrugs.

"It hasn't kicked in yet. Is Justin here?"

"I'm not sure." I tell her. "Do you want me to find out?"

"Yeah, I want to at least know he's showing up." She laughs nervously. I slip out of the room and walk across the hall, knocking loudly.

I hear a bunch of men shouting and then silence.

A moment later, the lock clicks and nobody opens the door.

What the hell!

I knock louder.

After a few seconds of me listening to them whisper argue, the lock clicks again and the door opens a crack, a familiar eye peeking out.

"Yes?" Danny asks.

"What is wrong with you?" I ask patiently.

"We thought it was Megan." Danny says, opening the door wider. He peeks across the hall at the open door and then grabs my arm, yanking me inside and slamming it shut again. Danny's cousins are all staring at me, along with Justin, Megan's groom, and Danny's Uncle's, Caleb and Caleb's father, along with a few men that must be Justin's family. "So what did you need?"

"Nothing, never mind." I say, opening the door.

"You needed something. What is it?" Justin asks.

"Nothing, I got all the information I needed."

"Dude, your wife is going to do something crazy." Justin whispers. "Do something about it!"

Danny hesitates and reaches for me to throw me over his shoulder, but I put my hand up.

"Don't."

He hesitates and then stuffs his hands in his pockets.

"Oh come on!" Justin laughs. "Pussy!"

"I'm not a pussy." Danny says. "It's called respecting my wife. She doesn't want me to do it, so I'm not doing it."

"It's true boy." One of the men I don't know says, putting his hand on Justin's shoulder. "If you piss off the wife, you're screwed."

Danny leans forward and kisses me, and then I slip back out of the door and across the hall.

"Well?" Megan asks.

"He's here."

She nods slowly.

"Alright."

Megan's wedding party is simple. The best man is my husband, and the two groomsmen are Jackson and Christian, Megan's brothers. Megan's maid of honor is me, and the bridesmaids are my cousin Abby and Danny and Megan's cousin from Kentucky, Brecklyn. She was at Danny and I's wedding too, but she wasn't in the wedding party because I wasn't close enough with her.

Since our wedding though, Megan moved to South Carolina with Justin, but they won't live together. They're only about two hours south of Danny and I in North Carolina, so we hang out a lot on the weekends. Justin and Danny got close, and Abby moved to North Carolina and stayed with our Grandma and Grandpa, and then she got her own apartment. Danny's Nana and Papa live in Virginia.

It seems like a lot has changed, but it really hasn't been much.

Justin's Mom and Grandma walk out for a moment and the second she's gone, Megan jumps up and locks the door, trapping all of us in the room with Beatrice, Megan's Mom Isabelle, Danny and Megan's Aunt Marie, Brecklyn, Abby, Danny and Megan's Grandma, and myself.

"I want to run." She whispers.

"What?" I ask loudly. She shushes me frantically with tears in her eyes.

"I can't marry him! He's not even good at kissing!"

"Okay sweetheart," Isabelle says to her daughter. "Let's all just calm down."

"No." Megan whispers. "I can't marry him! I just don't love him! I said yes because I wanted to get married but the closer the minute gets, I don't want to marry him!"

Everyone looks at me.

"What are you looking at me for?" I whisper shout.

"You got nervous before you married Danny." Megan grips my hands. "Did you think about running?"

I sigh.

"No." I say honestly. "I thought about running away with Danny and eloping, but never about running away without Danny."

"What do you guys think? Should I run?"

Everyone is silent, exchanging glances, and they all look back at me.

I sigh.

"Meg, when in doubt, get the fuck out."

We all just kind of look at each other in this intense silence.

"Okay, um, everyone else got rental cars or got Uber's here." She says shakily. "Grace, you're the only one with a private vehicle."

I swear under my breath.

"What? What is it?" Brecklyn asks.

"My husband has the keys!"

"Well...fuck!" Megan gasps.

I reach for the door handle but everyone starts whispering no and running to stop me at the same time.

"Relax. I'll get the keys from him."

"You can't tell him." Everyone says in sync.

"My son can't lie for shit. He can't know." Beatrice says.

"Why do I have to lie to him?" I whisper.

"Because it's your car!"

I press my hands against my face and nod frantically.

"Alright, okay, fine. We get the keys, go to my house and make a plan. We have about...ten minutes probably to get a plan before phones start ringing. Gather your shit and we can climb out that window." I point to the window. Beatrice walks over to it and pushes it open.

I run my hands down my face and take a deep breath, putting on my best lie face. I open the door to the bridal room and walk across the hall, knocking loudly.

After a moment, Danny opens the door.

"Yes?"

"I need the keys." I say.

"Why?" He asks.

"I forgot my phone in the car." I lie flatly.

He sighs.

"Okay, but put them in your purse. I don't want to carry them."

"Alright, fine."

I take the keys from him and dart forward to kiss him, and then I walk across the hall and shut the door.I grab my purse and we all dart towards the window.

At the last second, Megan grabs the wedding dress of the couch.

I throw myself through the window first and run in heels through the luscious green grass to my black Jeep Grand Cherokee. Ocean broke a couple of months ago so we got a new one.

I unlock the car and get in, turning the engine on.

A moment later, Danny's Grandma comes running to my car and I watch as Aunt Megan comes, and then Aunt Isabelle, and then Abby, and then Brecklyn, and then Megan, and then Beatrice.

The car fits five but we've managed to shove eight people in here.

"We need a plan." Megan says shakily. "Somebody is going to find me. I need somewhere to hide."

"You don't need anywhere to hide." I say calmly. "We go to Danny and I's house and we don't leave or let anybody in."

"Unless it's a Grey." Abby says.

"Right." I nod.

We go rushing out of the parking lot and out to the street.

I turn left and go over the bridge, and then turn left again.

I hurry down the road and drive up the driveway, pulling into the garage.

I shut the garage door and get out, rushing inside.

Everyone follows me up the stairs to the main floor. I go lock all the doors and windows.

"God, do you have any alcohol?" Megan asks.

"I don't drink."

Megan sits down on the couch and buries her head in her hands.

"I can't believe we just left him at our wedding." She mutters.

*****

This chapter had me cracking up!

Also, how many of you want to see pictures of Danny and Grace's house?

~Sam

Chapter Two: Doorbells Ringing

The pic on the side is of Grace and Danny's house. The AN on the bottom has more info!

*****

Chapter Two: Doorbells Ringing

I hear the doorbell ringing insistently and we all exchange glances.

I realize that, because it's my house, I have to get the door.

It's been an hour since we got to my house and we've spent the whole time panicking and we tried to go down to the boardwalk to look across the water, but we couldn't see anything for the wedding because it wasn't next to the water.

But now whoever it ringing it hitting the button angrily.

I take a deep breath to prepare myself and walk over to the door. I unlock it and open it a crack.

My husband looks pissed. He's with his cousins, Caleb, his Grandpa, Megan's Dad Logan, Uncle Kevin, Brecklyn's husband Jared, and their baby Preston.

I pull the door open and they all come flooding into the house.

I shut the door quickly and lock it.

Danny immediately rounds on me.

"You lied to me. You ditched me at the park! And locked me out of my own house!"

I walk past him to the living room where all the girls are standing.

Megan stands up, running her hands across her face.

"Well? Does he know?"

"Uh, yeah, he knows." Uncle Logan says.

"He tried to kill me." Danny seethes. "Because I'm his best man and my wife was driving the get away car!"

"Oh get over it, Daniel." Beatrice says.

"No, because he could have busted my face in!"

"But he didn't." I say.

"You just ditched me! And then locked me out!"

"She did it to everyone." Caleb says. "Calm down."

"It was my fault." Megan says.

"But you didn't lie to me." Danny says, frustrated.

Brecklyn sighs and takes her baby from her husband Jared.

"I'm sorry." I say. "I'm glad he didn't hurt you."

Danny sighs, rubbing his forehead.

"Why?" He finally asks Megan.

"Yeah, you guys seemed happy, and he's really nice." Logan says to his daughter.

"I don't love him, Dad." Megan says. "I can't marry him. I can't."

Danny sighs and sinks onto the couch, putting his arm over his eyes.

"Something tells me this is going to be a very long day." He mutters.

*****

The entire day was spent listening to the doorbell go off and choosing to ignore it. We laid around and watched movies and Megan would cry at anything. The sun has vanished hours ago but nobody got up to cook, so Danny and I ordered six pizzas.

"Next time somebody comes to the door, I'm answering it." I announce to everyone.

"That's a bad idea." Megan says.

"I'm tired of listening to the doorbell. They're going to break the machine. I'm answering it and telling them to screw off."

"The guy just got left at the altar." Abby mutters. "Have some compassion."

"Well I'm not going to be a bitch to the guy." I say. "But I'm going to tell him she's leaving him and ask him to stop ringing the bell."

I stand up and start collecting plates from everyone, and Beatrice follows me to the kitchen to clean them.

"So." She says.

"So?" I ask.

"So when are you guys having a baby."

I sigh.

Danny and I have been married for a year and eight months and since the six month mark, everyone has been asking us when we're having a baby.

They're all so desperate for fresh Grey blood.

I always tell them I don't know, but honestly...we've been trying for eight months. We agreed after we moved in and furnished the house that we would start trying after a year of being married.

We've been trying for eight months with no luck, and I've gone to the doctor for it and he's gone to the doctor for it and we're both fertile.

I've spent many days and nights crying hysterically about it. Every time my period is late, I get excited. Every time I get a cramp, I get excited.

I was hoping to be eight months pregnant by now, but I'm not pregnant at all.

"Grace?" She asks.

"I don't know." I say.

"Aw come on." She says.

"I really just don't know." I say seriously.

"Well alright." She mutters.

We clean all the dishes, dry them, and put them away, and then we go back to the living room.

It hurts me when they ask because I see the hope in their eyes, and then it vanishes.

Beatrice is the only one that keeps asking, but nobody has asked us why we're waiting.

I sit down next to Danny, dropping my head on my shoulder.

It's December and it gets really cold here at night. There's usually frost in the morning. It usually snows in very late December through February. Around this time of year, I avoid going onto the dock. It's just too cold, and I don't go outside without the sun, because it's freezing.

Danny rubs my arm gently and I sigh against him.

I hate myself for wanting everyone to leave, but I want to cry about not having a baby.

The doorbell rings and everyone groans.

This time, I stand up, marching to the door.

I pause to remind myself to be nice, and then I reach for the handle.

I pull open the front door, my eyes wandering around for a moment before I see movement below me. I look down, coming face to face with a little boy with messy blonde hair and brown eyes. A small Spider-Man suitcase is next to him.

"Hi." He says. "Are you Gracelyn?"

What the hell?

"Yes." I say slowly, my eyes darting around for a parent. I crouch in front of him. "Where is your Mommy? Or your Daddy?"

"I'm Micah! You're my big sister!"

He darts forward, his arms wrapping around my legs.

What the fuck what the fuck what the fuck!

"Daniel!" I call, awkwardly patting the back of the child. He's in a short sleeve shirt and shorts. There's no coat on him and it's in the low thirties. His lips are blue and he looks like he's freezing.

I hear hurried footsteps.

"What?" Danny asks.

I pry the boy off of me and turn to him.

"Uh..." he trails off, rubbing his neck.

"How old are you?" I ask the little boy.

"I'm five and three quarters." The little boy says in his baby voice.

I look into his eyes and they're the same eyes that I looked into when I pulled the child out of the street.

I slowly walk onto the porch and grab his suitcase. I feel all the blood draining out of my face as I walk into the house with Micah, shutting the door slowly.

He smiles up at me and I smile back awkwardly, walking slowly into the living room. He trails behind me and Danny trails behind him.

"Did you get rid of him?" Megan asks.

"What's wrong with you?" Beatrice stands up.

Micah walks around the couch and he looks a little jittery.

Everyone gets silent, and then the TV shuts off.

I mean, yeah, there's a chance that this is my brother, and he has the same name...

"What's your last name?" I ask him.

"Lewinsky." He smiles.

"You mean Levinsky?" I ask.

"That's what I said."

I rub my forehead, my hands shaking slightly.

"Okay, uh...what's your middle name?"

"Andrew."

Fuck! That's my Dad's middle name.

"Okay." I say carefully.

"Grace?" Danny whispers. "Is this-"

"My name is Micah. I'm five and three quarters." He says to Danny.

"Oh good lord." Caleb mutters.

"What's your Mom's name?"

"Eileen." He says. "My Dad is Scott. I don't like my Mom because she's really mean, but my Dad is nice."

"Micah, this is my husband Danny. You stay with him for a minute, okay?"

"Yeah." He says.

I walk down the hall, increasing in speed as I go until I reach the half bathroom.

I don't even shut the door, I just start throwing up.

As I kneel on the floor hacking my stomach out, I only have one thought.

This is reaching out?!

*****

Lmao so I know the pictures of the house may not have satisfied your needs, so if you send me a PM, I'll give you the address

~Sam

Chapter Three: Burning Water

I made a typo last chapter. Micah is five and three quarters, not four and three quarters. It was fixed and changed in this chapter

*****

Chapter Three: Burning Water

"Micah, this is my husband Danny. You stay with him for a minute, okay?"

"Yeah." He says.

I walk down the hall, increasing in speed as I go until I reach the half bathroom.

I don't even shut the door, I just start throwing up.

As I kneel on the floor hacking my stomach out, I only have one thought.

This is reaching out?!

I throw up until I'm dry heaving and then I flush the toilet and brush my teeth crazily, and then I glare at the sink for a minute or two, clear my throat, and walk back into the living room.

"Did you throw up? I heard you throwing up." Micah says.

"No, I was coughing." I lie. I grab his backpack and unzip it.

There's a paper on top of his stuff with my Dad's messy handwriting. The bag smells like my parents house. I bury my head in my hands, shaking my head.

This is absurd!

All that is written on the paper is a phone call and the words do not call unless it's between 10PM and 5AM

I look at the clock.

10:23PM.

I grab my phone from my back pocket and dial, my hands shaking.

It rings three times and stops.

"Hello?" Dad asks.

"What the fuck!" I whisper shout, standing up. I walk into the kitchen, ripping my fingers through my hair.

"Oh, hey Grace."

"Dad!" I say loudly. "What the hell!"

"So he got there okay?"

"Uh yeah, he got here okay! This is what you call reaching out?!"

"Of course not." He says. "But I don't have a choice."

I hear Danny saying something to his parents and then he walks into the kitchen. I grab his hand and pull him through the kitchen to the laundry room, slamming the door. I put it on speaker.

"What do you mean you don't have a choice?" I ask angrily.

"I don't have anybody else, Gracelyn. I had to jump through multiple hoops to find you."

"You better start explaining." Danny says.

I hear him sigh.

"Eileen and I are in a full swing custody battle and because of her history with abuse, Micah can't stay with us. They said he has to stay with somebody until somebody wins the case or they will provide temporary housing, like a foster home."

"So what? Your plan was to dump your son on us?" I ask. "Are you fucking crazy?"

"Grace, I don't have another choice." He says.

"And what the hell happens when Mom's finds out he's with me?" I ask.

"She won't find out." He says.

"Scott, custody battles can last months." Danny says.

"There are papers I've signed that give you guys temporary custody." He says. "So you can keep him and enroll him in school..." he trails off.

"No." I say. "No, absolutely not. We have-have lives, Dad! Jobs!"

"Do you have children?" He asks.

"No, but-"

"While you're at work you can take him to a babysitter. My parents live near you. Send him to them."

"I can't believe this. I can't fucking believe this."

"He's not that hard to watch. He's potty trained. He can talk. Just sit with him in the tub and feed him."

"How did he even get to us?" Danny asks angrily.

"I paid a guy to take a plane with him and then uber to your house. He stayed in the car until you answered the door."

"And what if they took him to the wrong house?!" I snap.

"You would leave a five year old out in the cold?"

"Micah is smart." Dad sighs. "Listen, I don't have a choice. It was either that or I drive out there and talk to you guys in person. With Eileen. Is that what you want?"

"Dad, I'm not raising your son. I told you to give him up for adoption! I told you that bitch was going to hurt him, and did you listen? No! You never fucking listen!"

"Okay, yes, you're right, but I love him. He's your brother, Gracelyn. Please do this for me. I'll pay you."

"It's not the money I'm worried about!" I snarl.

"If you guys really can't watch him, send him home and I'll find somebody else to watch him."

I bury my head in my hands.

"We'll call you back." Danny hangs up on him.

I immediately turn and bury my head in his chest.

I can hear Micah talking in the living room.

We stay silent for a few minutes and we just stand there in a long hug.

"If we send him back, my Mom knows where he is." I whisper, pulling away. "He's only five, Danny. He's practically a baby."

He rests his chin on my head.

"Grace." He murmurs. "If we do this, we can't have a baby. You know that, right? We need to start using condoms again until your Dad comes to pick him up. It's too much."

I nod into his chest.

"It's not working anyways." I mutter.

We're both silent and I want to cry.

"So we're keeping him." I whisper, pulling away.

His eyes search mine for a long time.

"Sweetheart, I don't think we have a choice. It's either this or a foster home."

I look down, nodding.

"Alright." I murmur. "Let's call my Dad back."

I pick up the phone and hit the number, putting it on speaker.

It rings once and then stops.

"Hello?"

"We'll keep him." I tell my Dad. "What time does he go to bed?"

"He doesn't have a bedtime."

I hesitate.

"Okay, is he in a booster seat?"

"Nope."

"Well what are his grades like?"

"I don't know."

I put my hand on my mouth.

"Alright. Did he eat dinner?"

"I don't know."

"Lunch?"

"Maybe. He didn't eat breakfast though. He said he wasn't hungry."

He isn't taking care of him.

I pinch the bridge of my nose and nod slowly.

"Okay."

"Alright. Oh Grace?"

"Yes?"

"He has nightmares."

I stare at my phone for a long time and start shaking my head.

"Alright, bye."

I hang up on him and lean against the counter.

"They aren't taking care of him, Danny." I whisper.

"Well don't worry. We will. Come on, let's go talk to him."

I shove my phone in my pocket and walk out of the laundry room. Everyone is watching Micah play on the floor.

He has one toy, a tiny little hot wheels car.

I walk to his suitcase and start digging through it, I pull out two pairs of underwear, one of them has holes in it. He has a pair of shorts and one shirt that has a bleach stain on it.

There are no pajamas and no other toys.

"Micah, is this all of your stuff?"

"Yes." He says.

I sit down on the coffee table and bury my head in my hands.

"Have you eaten today?" Danny asks him.

"I had four crackers on the airplane." He says.

"Come here." I tell him.

He sets his toy down on the table and walks over to me. I grab his shirt and lift it up.

I can count each one of his ribs.

And he stinks.

"When is the last time you had a bath?" I ask, dropping his shirt.

He shrugs.

"I don't know. A few weeks probably.

A few weeks.

I mean, this is ridiculous! He doesn't even have any warm clothes to sleep in!

"Are you mad at me?" He whispers.

And then he starts backing away from me, and he looks scared.

"I'm sorry I don't have more stuff." He mumbles.

I don't know what to do. I don't know what to say, I just stare at him, shocked.

And I think about the position he's in, and I've been there, and I know how he feels.

When is the last time this little boy got hugged by somebody? When was he last loved by anyone?

I used to spend hours in my room hiding from the demon that scarred this baby.

"Micah, I'm not Mom." I say finally. "I won't hurt you. I know it's hard for you to trust me, but I promise I will never, ever hurt you on purpose."

He hesitates.

"Okay." He finally says.

"Now, Danny is going to make you something to eat, and we're going to get you in the bathtub, okay?"

His eyes light up when he realizes he gets to take a bath.

"Okay."

I look at Danny and he nods. I put Micah's things back in his bag and go upstairs. He follows me.

We go upstairs and I turn to the right, walking into the master bedroom. I shut the door behind me and he follows me into the bathroom.

I'm not sure how hot Micah likes the water so I have him feel it first, and then I pour in bubbles and plug the drain.

We have a jacuzzi tub but it might be too deep for him, so I make it about as deep as the width from my wrist to my elbow and then I shut the water off.

"Go on and climb in." I tell him.

He takes off his shirt and I try not to stare at how thin he is.

Yeah, Danny and I are definitely going to fatten him up.

When he reaches for his pants, I walk out and go into the jack and jill bathroom attached to the two guest rooms across the house. I get an unused toothbrush and go into the bedroom. I dig through my drawer and get the thickest long sleeve shirt I have, and I check to make sure the pair of underwear he has without holes are clean, and then I walk into the bedroom.

He has his car in the tub with him, racing around the walls.

"If you're my sister, what is your husband to me?" He asks, pausing the car noises he's making with his mouth to look at me.

"He would be your brother-in-law." I reply.

"So do I just call him Danny?" He asks.

"Yes." I nod.

He goes back to playing with his car, and I set a timer on my phone for ten minutes.

I sit there while he plays, and when the timer goes off, I silence it and grab the bar of soap.

"You need to wash up now." I tell him.

"Okay." He takes a deep breath and goes underwater, coming back up with his hair sopping wet. I smile and put soap on the washcloth. I hand it to him.

"I don't know how." He says.

"You've never washed yourself before?" I asks slowly.

"I don't think I've ever been washed."

I stare at him for a long time, and then I nod my head.

"Okay, take it." I hand him the washcloth and he takes it in his hand. "Now you just rub it everywhere except for your hair. Keep your eyes closed when you get it on your face or you will get soap in your eyes and it will hurt."

I watch him as he washes his whole body, and I put more soap on when he needs it. After the first time, I make him sit back down and then wash again, and then I grab Danny's shampoo, because mine smells like strawberries. I put a little on my hand.

"Close your eyes." I tell him.

He does as I say and I lean forward, rubbing the soap all into his hair. He holds still, and after a couple moments, I stop and send him under water to rinse his hair out.

When he's all clean, I pull the plug to the drain.

I take his hands and help him climb out of the tub, and he uses his hands to cover his private parts.

"Don't look." He says.

"I'm not looking." I say, getting a towel for him. I wrap it around his body and rub my hands up and down his arms.

After a few seconds, I help him dry off the rest of his body and then his hair. He puts his underwear on and I help him into my shirt. It goes down to his knees. I dry off his car and hand it to him.

"Go downstairs to Danny, okay?"

"Yes." He replies, walking out of the bathroom and out of the bedroom.

I clean up the mess and put his dirty clothes in the hamper, walking downstairs.

Micah is standing in front of the kitchen table watching Danny set his food down.

"Can I have some coffee please?" He asks Danny, who starts choking on air.

"What?" Danny asks.

"Coffee. Mommy lets me drink it black."

Danny gives me an astounded look.

"Micah, little boys don't drink coffee." Danny says slowly.

My brother hesitates. "So what am I supposed to drink?"

"Water. Milk. Chocolate milk. Apple juice."

Micah looks shocked.

"I want water." He says.

"How do you ask?" Danny replies.

Micah hesitates.

"Please."

"Please what?"

"Please give me water."

"No, you say 'may I please have some water?'" Danny corrects him.

"May I please have some water?"

"Yes you may." Danny says, giving me a shocked look as he walks back to the kitchen.

He comes back with a plastic cup of water. Our family is watching the ordeal and some of them are standing around the kitchen.

"Thank you." Micah says.

"You're welcome." Danny replies. He sits down across from Micah and I sit next to Danny, watching Micah take a sip of the water.

He swallows it.

"Wow!" He exclaims. "The kind my Mom gives me makes me throat burn!"

My hand slaps over my mouth.

No. There's no way.

Danny's jaw is half open.

"Can I talk to you please?" I ask Danny. "In private?"

Before he can answer, I'm dragging him out of the kitchen. Beatrice and Caleb go into the kitchen to watch him while we're gone, and I was planning on going to the laundry room again but I feel sick, so I start dragging him to the bathroom.

The moment I get in there, I start puking again. I hear the bathroom door shut and his hands in my hair, and when I've thrown up with him in the past he usually will say something to try and make me feel better, but tonight he stays silent.

After a moment, I stop and flush the toilet, and then I brush my teeth and slide my back down the door until I sit on the floor.

"He told me he has never been washed before. He didn't know how to wash him." I whisper.

"He thought the water was vodka!" Danny whisper shouts. "I mean-neither one of them should be getting any custody! Look at that little boys ribcage! You can count them!"

"And he never uses a booster seat! What the hell!"

"Alright, okay, tomorrow he gets enrolled in school, he goes with us shopping to get him clothes and stuff, he goes to the doctor...I mean, this little boy knows nothing!"

"Grace." He looks me dead in the eye. "I love you to death, but if you let your father walk away with Micah, I-I-" he cuts off, running his hands over his mouth. "I will never look at you the same again."

"Danny, we can't raise him." I whisper.

"Well neither can your Dad." He snaps.

"We can find somebody to raise him. Somebody close." I say. "But no matter what, he doesn't go to my parents. Agreed?"

"Agreed." He stands up and offers his hand down to me. I take it, allowing him to pull me off the floor. "I love you, baby, but this little boy deserves so much better than your parents."

"I agree one hundred percent." I reply.

We exit the bathroom and go back to the breakfast area where Micah is eating grilled cheese and drinking his water.

I pull up a chair next to him and sit down.

"Micah, from now on, you will have a bath every other day." I tell him.

"Okay." He says.

"You will go to sleep at eight every night."

"Why?" He asks.

"Because you're a kid." Danny says. "And kids sleep early."

"Alright." Micah shrugs.

"You will be responsible for cleaning your own room."

His face lights up.

"I'm going to have my own room?!" He exclaims.

"Yes. Didn't you have your own room in Florida?"

"No, I got to sleep on the couch." He says.

We're all quiet.

"You will eat all three meals, and when you get hungry, you have to promise to tell us." Danny says.

"Okay, I promise."

"Tomorrow we're going to get you more clothes and a seat for the car."

"I get clothes?" He whispers. "Can I have my own jacket?"

I look down, my heart aching for this little baby.

"Yes honey, you can have your own jacket." I whisper.

"So I get to eat whenever I want?" He asks. "And have my own bedroom? With my own bed? And I get more clothes?"

"Yeah." I say sadly, because that's normal for every other kid.

But to him, it's like Christmas.

*****

This is sad. Really sad

~Sam

Chapter Four: Breakfast

The pic on the side is of Micah because somebody asked for it and I forgot to post it

*****

Chapter Four: Breakfast

I lay in bed in the middle of the night, staring at the ceiling. Danny's arm is around my waist, his leg thrown over both of mine, his head nestled as close to me as he can get. His parents and grandparents are down the hall, his Aunt Isabelle and Uncle Logan are in one room downstairs and Aunt Marie and Uncle Kevin are in another room downstairs. Brecklyn, Jared, and the baby are in the room in the basement and Megan, Jackson, and Christian are sharing the living room. We blew up our queen sized blowup mattress and Megan is sharing it with Jackson. The two older siblings forced their little brother to take the couch.

And Micah is sleeping on the couch in Danny and I's sitting room in our bedroom.

But as I lie here at three in the morning, I feel sick.

How did my Dad let this get so bad? Was today really the first time somebody ever washed Micah? Why doesn't he have any clothes? And Micah said the water burned. Was my Mom giving my brother vodka?

And he doesn't eat apparently. The little boy is a stick.

I really don't feel like going to sleep because I know if I fall asleep I'm going to have horrible nightmares.

I worm my way out of Danny's grasp and grab my winter coat. I already have on thick pajama pants. I stuff my feet in my fur boots and pull my coat on. I slip out of the bedroom and walk down the stairs, stopping at the linen closet to grab a throw blanket. I walk carefully around Megan and Jackson's blowup mattress, walking out to the balcony. I shut the door silently behind me and walk down the path to the boardwalk on the right. It's freezing out here so I wrap the blanket around my shoulders.

When I get closer to the end, I see a small figure standing there, looking down at the water.

I hesitate.

Who the hell?

"Micah?" I ask when I get closer.

He's standing at the edge shivering, his arms wrapped around his little body.

He's only wearing my shirt and I know he must be freezing.

The boardwalk has a little roof over it to block the rain and sometimes in the summers I like to sit under it while it's raining and paint. There's a bench around it, so I walk over to him and put my hand on his shoulder.

He jumps and starts to fall forward, but I catch his small body with my arms, and then he starts crying.

I pull him over to one of the benches and wrap the blanket around his body, pulling him against my side.

He cuddles against me and I can feel him shaking.

I pick him up and carry him up to the house. I go up the stairs and onto the main floor, shutting the door.

I take him into the laundry room and shut the door, turning the light on.

His little arms are around my neck and his legs are around my waist. I sit him on the dryer and stand in front of him, rubbing his back as he cries.

And I relate to him. To a little boy who is five years old.

I know why he's awake. He had a nightmare. He's crying because he had a nightmare.

This little baby is devastated and scared and heartbroken.

So I don't say anything, I just hold him, rubbing his back and running my fingers through his hair.

After a while, he stops crying, but we don't say anything for a few minutes.

Finally, he pulls away and looks up at me with a red face.

"Did Mom ever hurt you?" He whispers.

I gently wipe away some wetness on his face, and I want to shield him from the truth, but he's smart and was forced to grow up.

"Yeah buddy, she did."

He looks down.

"Gracie?" He whispers.

"Yes?"

"I wish I was never born sometimes. Mommy doesn't love me. Nobody does. She always hurt me. I wanted to stay at school."

"I love you, Micah." I whisper.

"You do?" He asks, and he gets a smile on his face.

"Of course I do. You're my little brother."

He smiles, and then it fades.

"Grace, I don't want to live with Mom and Dad ever again."

"I know buddy, you won't."

"Do you promise?"

What if the court decides he goes to my Dad no matter what?

"I'm going to try my hardest to keep you away from them." I whisper.

"Okay." He says. "I don't want to go back to sleep today."

"You don't have to." I tell him.

*****

I took him upstairs after a little while and I laid with him while he was on the couch. After a while, he fell asleep cuddled to me and I didn't want to leave him there, so I fell asleep too.

Now he's sitting at the dining table with a plate full of eggs and bacon and sausage and pancakes and he has a huge glass of orange juice. The rest of the family is at the dining table too, and I have a whole plate in front of me but I just can't eat. I'm not hungry at all. Everything smells good, but I just don't want to eat.

"Grace, aren't you going to eat?" Danny asks.

"Yeah, no, I'm not hungry." I sigh.

"But you haven't eaten since dinner." Beatrice says.

"Maybe you're pregnant." Danny's Aunt Isabelle says hopefully.

"Oh, I hope so. You guys do want kids, right?"

Danny and I exchange glances but either one of us answer them.

"Well you have been holding your tits a lot." Brecklyn mutters. "When I got pregnant with Preston, my first sign was clothes being too tight, and then my boobs hurt, and then I just had no desire to eat for two days." She shrugs.

"I'm not pregnant." I say. "I'm just not hungry."

"Well maybe you are pregnant and you just don't know yet." Beatrice says.

"Yeah, when are you supposed to start your period?" Danny's Grandma asks.

I pinch the bridge of my nose.

"I don't know. Can we just drop it? I'm not pregnant!"

"Well you threw up twice yesterday." Abby says.

"Sweetheart, when is the last time you got your period?" Danny asks slowly.

I rub my eyebrow and sigh, thinking.

I know I didn't get it last month but my period is always irregular and I sometimes skip some months. That happened ever since my Mom's abuse. The doctor told me it was stress.

I think back to October and I remember having enough blood for a panty liner but not enough for a tampon, and it was a weird color, not the normal red, but a very light pink.

Does that count?

When was my last full, real period?

Without a word, I push my chair back and stand up from the table, walking out of the dining room.

I hurry up the stairs and the closer I get to the safety of my bedroom, the sicker I feel.

I just make it to the toilet and start throwing up again.

This is the most I've thrown up in years!

I flush the toilet and brush my teeth, staring at myself in the mirror.

I pull my shirt up to look at my breasts in my bra, and they're spilling out. The bra doesn't even fit.

I turn to the side, breathing heavily with nerves, and there isn't a bump. My belly is still flat and it looks the same, but my breasts are sore and larger. On top of that, I can see the veins leading into my breasts clearly, when usually, I can't.

So I was spotting in October, around the time of Abby's twenty sixth birthday. Actually, it was the morning of her birthday. October fourteenth. A Saturday.

That was when I was supposed to start my period. I remember that day because when I saw the light pink on the toilet paper, I started crying because it meant I wasn't pregnant.

Last month it never came because of stress, and this month it should have come around the fourteenth, but it's the seventeenth and it's still not here.

And my boobs are really sore, but I figured they were sore because of my period.

But if I take that test and it's negative, I'm going to cry. A lot.

I hear footsteps and the sound of the bedroom door opening and closing, and then my husband walks into the bathroom.

I sit down on the edge of the tub and just look at him

"Grace-"

"Danny, my last period was in September." I whisper, my hands shaking slightly. "The dress didn't fit because of my boobs, they've been sore and my bra is too small." I lift my shirt up to show him.

"So...do you think you're pregnant?"

I drop my head into my hands and sigh.

"I don't want to get my hopes up. If I take the test and it's negative, I-" I cut off. "I'm going to be heartbroken."

"If you take the test and it's positive, you're going to be thrilled." He crouches down to my level and puts his hands on my knees. "And you have to take it either way."

I reach down and hold both of his hands in mine.

"I'll pee on it and we can leave it on the counter and look at it after we go shopping for Micah."

"Or you pee on it and we can look now." He says. "And then I can make sure you're not overworking yourself if you are pregnant."

"Danny." I whisper shakily. "I'm scared."

"Me too." He murmurs, rubbing his thumbs across the back of my finger. "It hurts me just as much as it hurts you every time it's negative." He whispers. "But if that test comes out positive..." he trails off. "It's going to be one of the best days of my life."

Neither one of us moves for a little while and then I stand up, walking over to the cabinet.

I told Danny last time that after we used the last test, I wasn't buying another one until I was certain I needed it.

I pull it out of the drawer and rip open the little foil packet.

"No matter what the result is, we don't tell anybody, okay? Not for a while at least."

"Okay." He murmurs.

We bought the expensive tests that tell you how far along you are. I pull the cap off of the test and walk over to the toilet. He follows me and as I pull my pants down, I look at him.

"I'm scared."

"Just go pee." He says, leaning against the doorframe to the small toilet room.

With a sigh, I pee on the stick and then shove the cap back on. I clean up, pull my pants up and flush, and then I walk over to the counter and set the test down. I wash my hands and dry them, and then I peek at the test. It's flashing the hourglass signal and I'm so nervous.

"God, I'm terrified." I mumble.

Danny wraps his arms around me and I wrap mine around his waist.

"Everything is going to be fine. If the test is negative, we'll keep trying and after the year, we'll go back to the doctor and talk about taking hormones or something. We're going to have a baby either way."

"Okay." I whisper.

We pull apart and look down at the test. I keep my hands over my mouth from nerves, looking at the test flash the hourglass sign. Danny stands beside me, rubbing his neck nervously.

I know we probably shouldn't stare at it but I can't look away.

It keeps flashing.

And flashing.

And flashing.

And then after what feels like an hour, it stops flashing.

Pregnant3+

*****

I'm very happy

~Sam

Chapter Five: Surprise Visitor

With a sigh, I pee on the stick and then shove the cap back on. I clean up, pull my pants up and flush, and then I walk over to the counter and set the test down. I wash my hands and dry them, and then I peek at the test. It's flashing the hourglass signal and I'm so nervous.

"God, I'm terrified." I mumble.

Danny wraps his arms around me and I wrap mine around his waist.

"Everything is going to be fine. If the test is negative, we'll keep trying and after the year, we'll go back to the doctor and talk about taking hormones or something. We're going to have a baby either way."

"Okay." I whisper.

We pull apart and look down at the test. I keep my hands over my mouth from nerves, looking at the test flash the hourglass sign. Danny stands beside me, rubbing his neck nervously.

I know we probably shouldn't stare at it but I can't look away.

It keeps flashing.

And flashing.

And flashing.

And then after what feels like an hour, it stops flashing.

Pregnant

3+

My hand grabs Danny's, holding on tightly. I blink a couple of times and move my face closer to the test, making sure the word not isn't anywhere on the digital screen.

But all it says it pregnant 3+

I look at my husband who's jaw is half opened.

"You see it too, right?" I whisper.

He puts his fist against his mouth to stifle his grin.

"Grace! We're having a baby!" He whisper shouts.

"We're having a baby!" I reply, my eyes filling with tears. He starts laughing and lifts me into the air, kissing my face everywhere.

We both have tears and he's grinning and I'm grinning and we're trying to kiss each other's faces but we keep moving, so kiss his lips instead.

Afterwards while of this, he sets me down, a giant smile on both of our faces.

"Okay, okay, when was your first missed period. We need to figure that out first."

"Okay." I laugh a little and shakily grab my phone from the pocket of my sweatpants. I go online and google a due date calculator. "Um...I think I was supposed to start on October fourteenth." I say. "So I should put that, right?"

"Yes." He smiles.

I type on October fourteenth of this year and watch as my phone load.

I'm due July twenty first.

"Okay, so that means I'm..." I start counting on my fingers. "Eight weeks."

"Right, okay." He laughs a little. "Okay, well you need to make a doctors appointment. We need to find the best OBGYN office in Wilmington."

I start Googling things and he and I agree on an office that has the best reviews on Google, and I call and make the appointment.

"When we go to the store, let's get more tests just to be sure, okay?" I say.

"Alright." He kisses my temple. "Let's keep this under wraps until we go to the doctor."

"Okay."

I take a deep breath to calm myself, put the positive test back into the drawer, and go downstairs.

Everyone is still at the table.

"So?" Abby asks. "Why were you guys up there for so long?"

"I was checking my app to see when my period is supposed to come." I lie smoothly. "It isn't supposed to come until the twenty eighth."

"But you missed last month." Beatrice says hopefully.

"No I didn't."

"Oh."

I feel the atmosphere switch to disappointment and I try to hide my smile.

"I still think you should eat." Beatrice says finally.

I genuinely don't want to, but what if our baby is hungry?

So I take my plate to the microwave and heat it back up, standing away from the microwave because of radiation and stuff.

When it goes off, I take my food back to the table.

"Jared and I are heading back to Kentucky with Preston today." Brecklyn says. "He has to work on Monday."

It's Saturday morning.

"So are Marie and I." Danny's Uncle Kevin announces.

"You guys don't have to rush out of here." Danny says.

"No, it's fine. We want to get home. There's supposed to be a winter storm coming through the southeast next week and we want to be home before it gets here."

I clear my throat.

"Meg, what are you going to do?"

She stabs a piece of her scrambled egg and sighs.

"I'm going back to South Carolina with Jackson and Christian. Mom and Dad are coming too. I don't want to go back to Michigan but Justin was all I really had in South Carolina."

"So why don't you move to Wilmington?" I ask, causing everyone to look at me. "You have Danny and I here, Abby and Kyle and Miley. You won't be alone."

"Yeah but I'm needy and when things break I make Justin fix it. I don't need to bother you guys with my problems-"

"Megan, you're not bothering us." Danny says.

She looks hesitant.

"Alright, I'll look into it." She says. "But for now I'm going back to South Carolina."

"We'll be back for Christmas, of course." Aunt Isabelle says.

"William and I are going back to Vermont." Grandma Jennifer announces.

Everyone looks at Beatrice and Caleb because they're the only ones that haven't announced any plans.

"Well actually, we wanted to talk to you guys." Caleb says, looking at Danny and I.

Uh oh.

"Oh?" I raise both eyebrows.

"Well the plan was...that, once you guys got pregnant-" Beatrice starts.

"Mom." Danny says.

She waves him off and keeps talking. "-We would move to wherever you guys were living to be nearby for the grandkids." She rests her hands on the table. "But it hasn't happened yet and...I don't know, I think it would be easier for us to move before you're expecting." She clears her throat. "So we wanted to move here and maybe possibly stay at your house until we're done renovating ours...assuming it will need renovations."

I rest my chin on my hands and look at my husband from across the table.

"Unless you guys don't want us moving here." Caleb says. "I understand not wanting your parents in your business while you're having kids."

It's going to be really helpful having them around with Danny and I and work and the new baby coming, especially if we still have Micah. We did just finish our last house and we could renovate theirs...

I look to my husband and I know he's thinking exactly what I'm thinking.

"Alright." He says slowly, waiting for me to nod or shake my head if I agree. I nod my head once. "But how is this working? Are you moving in before you have a house?"

"Well..." Caleb clears his throat. "It's going to be hard to look for a place while we're living in Florida."

"We can pay rent." Beatrice adds.

"We don't need money." Danny and I say in sync.

"Are you sure?" Beatrice asks. "Because now you have Micah to provide for."

Nobody really knows our financial status because it's not really any of their business, but everyone probably assumes we're wealthy from the look of our house.

"We're fine." Danny says

"Alright well then we're going to go back to Florida and pack our stuff up and we'll get a storage unit."

"Okay." I say.

*****

A few hours later, everyone was gone, so we put Micah in the car and went to Target. We got him his own soaps for the bath tub and a rack for him to put them on. We got him a lot of bath toys and actual toys to play with in the house, and a chest for him to put them in. We got a stool for the bathroom so he can reach the sink. He got a toothbrush and kids toothpaste, along without loofa to wash his body. We got him new bedsheets since he's in the queen bed in one of the guest rooms, but it has adult sheets on it. We bought him an entire new wardrobe, swim trunks, goggles for when he goes swimming, a booster seat for the car, a new backpack with folders, paper, pencils, crayons, and a pencil sharpener.

We also got three more pregnancy tests.

We stopped by Tropical Smoothie on the way home and got food for all of us, but I was so tired that I fell asleep the minute we left the drive through.

Danny made me get up when we got home and I fell asleep on the couch.

Now I feel a small hand on my shoulder, shaking me.

I stir slightly, forcing my eyes open.

Micah stands in front of me in his new clothes. His hair is damp and he's wearing pajamas. The scent of the dove soap we bought him earlier wafts up my nose.

"Danny told me to wake you up because Kyle and Miley are coming over for dinner."

I push myself into the upright position, rubbing my forehead.

And then I feel like I'm going to puke.

I dart around my brother and run down the hall to the bathroom. I kick the door shut and start throwing up, nearly missing the toilet.

I sit there for a minute and then flush and brush my teeth, walking to the kitchen where I can hear something sizzling on the stove.

"Hi." Danny says, flipping a steak on the pan.

"Hi." I reply.

"Did you sleep okay?" He asks, kissing my cheek. I nod.

The doorbell rings, causing me to kiss him quickly and walk to the front door. Micah follows behind me.

I unlock the door and pull it open, expecting to see Miley and Kyle, but it's not.

No, the person standing on my porch is my father.

Micah stands next to me.

"Hi Dad." He says.

"Hey bud." Dad says. He looks at me and raises his eyebrows. "Can I come in?"

What is he doing here?

Slowly, I step aside to let him in.

When he's inside, I shut the door. Dad looks around, his eyes lingering on Danny and I's wedding photograph on the wall in the dining room.

"Nice place you have here." He says.

"Thanks." I say slowly. I rub my forehead awkwardly and walk across the house to the kitchen. I hear him following me. "Danny." I whisper when I reach my husband.

He turns around, his eyebrows shooting up when he sees my Dad walking into the kitchen with Micah.

"Hey." Dad says like he just saw us yesterday.

Micah doesn't seem scared or jumpy around Dad.

"Is Mom here?" Micah asks.

"No, she's at home." He answers Micah.

Danny shuts the stove off.

"I'll be right back."

I shoot him an incredulous look but he walks out anyways.

Dad stays quiet and I pet Pepper's ears so I can look like I'm doing something.

After a minute, Danny comes back.

"Sorry." He says, moving to stand next to me.

"Dad, why are you here?" I ask bluntly.

He sighs.

"I need to talk to you guys...and Grandma and Grandpa, but it's important and I didn't want to do it on the phone."

"So you drove all the way to North Carolina?" I ask slowly.

"You drove all the way to Maryland to talk to your Mom." He reminds me.

"Fair enough." I sigh. "Let me go call Grandma."

*****

I honestly want to hear your theories on why he's there

~Sam

Chapter Six: Bubble Bath

Is there anything you guys want to see a picture of? Should I just make another Danny/Grace collage? Maybe post a pic of Grace's Dad? I hate not putting something up.

******

Chapter Six: Bubble Bath

I sit at the breakfast table next to my husband. We were having Miley and Kyle over, but now my Dad and Grandparents are here. None of us have spoken to him in a while, and my Grandparents are happy to meet their grandson but not so happy to see their son.

"Scott, why are you here?" Grandpa asks.

"Micah, how about you go play?" Dad asks him.

Micah looks down at his hands.

"I don't want to, Dad. I want to know what you're going to say."

"Just let the adults talk for now, alright? I'll tell you later." He says calmly.

Micah looks skeptical, and then he looks at me.

"Can I open up my toys?"

"Yeah." I nod.

Micah leaves the table and I'm just so confused.

Why is he being so nice to Micah? For somebody that's letting his son have alcohol, you would think he wouldn't be that nice.

Danny's hand finds mine under the table and Dad takes a deep breath.

The second I hear Micah's bedroom door shut, I break the silence.

"Why were you giving him alcohol?"

Dad sighs.

"What are you talking about?"

"We gave him water. He said the water he gets at your home burns his throat."

Silence.

"He said that?"

"Yes." I snap.

"I mean, what the hell Scott? You can count the boys ribs!" Grandma says.

"He said he never gets baths and he didn't know what washing himself in the bath was, because he had never done it before. He has two pairs of underwear that weren't ripped, shorts, one shirt with holes and one without. The boy is five years old and he thought that getting clothes that fit him was just like Christmas." I say angrily

"It's not me, Gracelyn. It's Eileen, you know that."

"No Dad, I don't know that." I stand up from the table. "Maybe if you didn't go back to her-"

"Oh for fucks sake, Gracelyn. That was six years ago!"

"Maybe if you didn't blame me for the shit she put me through-"

"I apologized for that." He sighs. "And I didn't know Eileen was giving him alcohol!"

"She's hurt him, Dad! He's five!"

"I didn't know!" He repeats.

"I don't believe you." I shake my head, and I feel sick. I put my hand on my stomach and shake my head. "I don't believe you at all. Why the hell are you here?"

"I'm here because Eileen buried the legal files that say you existed." He says, standing up from the table. "And my lawyer thinks she's going to win custody of Micah."

The house falls silent.

Grandpa runs his hands through his hair, Grandma puts her hand on her mouth, Danny looks pissed, and I brace myself against the table with both hands.

"So what's your plan?" I ask finally.

"My plan is to take him and run to another country." He stands up. "And that's why I'm here. I'm here to take Micah."

"Is the case going to trial?" I demand.

"Yes. They set the trial date to April twenty eighth."

"You're not taking Micah." I say.

"What?" He asks.

"You're not taking Micah."

"Grace, if I don't take Micah-"

"She's not going to win the case." I say. "I promise you that."

"You can't promise that."

"Well I am. She's not taking Micah."

"Yeah, because I'm taking him tonight."

"Dad, I'm pregnant." I blurt, running my hands across my face. Danny's eyebrows shoot up.

"What?" Dad asks.

"I'm pregnant, okay? If you take him to another country and the police come here, that means you've put me in the position where I have to lie for you. By the time the trial comes I'll be like six months along. If I lie and they find out a couple months later, they're going to send me and Danny to jail for concealing a kidnapping or something, and they're going to take our baby." I press my hands together and move closer to him. "Dad, I'm begging you, you can't run away with him. I will fix this, but I need you to stay in Florida." He looks hesitant. "Please just do this one thing for me." I whisper, my eyes full of tears.

There is a long silence before he speaks.

"Okay." He whispers. "Alright, I'll stay." He looks scared. "But you can't let her take Micah, Gracelyn. If she gets ahold of him-"

"If she gets ahold of him, he's going to end up dead." I whisper. "I know."

He nods slowly and pulls me into a hug. I hug him back and after a moment, he pulls away.

"You're really pregnant?"

"I tested positive for one test. I haven't had a chance to take any others, but you guys can't tell anybody okay? The only reason you know is so you don't ruin our life and our baby's life."

"Alright." He says. "I won't say anything."

"Thank you." I whisper.

*****

He wanted to stay the night but I flatly told him to stay with Grandma and Grandpa, and now I'm sitting in a bubble bath staring at the wall, trying to come up with a plan.

Danny hasn't said a word to me since I told my Dad I was pregnant, and after Dad left we sat in silence for a few minutes before I went upstairs. I threw up twice and then got in the tub, and now I'm sitting here with my knees against my chest, crying.

How am I going to save Micah? Am I going to even be a good mother?

I hear the bedroom door open and close and I use the water to wet my face.

A moment later, my husband walks into the bathroom.

He looks at the bubbly water and then pulls his shirt over his head.

"Micah is sleeping." He says, unbuttoning his jeans. He removes both his pants and his boxers, tossing all of this clothes in the dirty hamper. He gestures for me to scoot forward and slips into the water behind me.

He doesn't say anything else and I don't answer him. He cups water in his hands and pours it down my shoulders, and then he starts to massage my shoulders.

"Please say something." I whisper weakly.

His hands don't pause their movements at all, but I hear him sigh.

"If the police showed up here, would you lie to protect your Dad and risk our family? Because that's what you told your Dad."

I think about the situation, me being all pregnant and about to pop, or my brother going to Micah.

But then my brother might have to live with my Mom.

But then our baby could go into the system, which is just as bad, and Danny and I could go to prison. I shrug his hands off of me and turn around to face him.

"Don't do that." I whisper. "Don't make me pick."

"Our child could end up in the system."

"My brother could end up with my Mom!" I say angrily. "Both are equally horrible, so don't make me sit here and pick which one of them gets a terrible fate!"

He rubs his hands up and down his face and nods.

"You're right. That's not fair."

I rub my temples.

"I need you to pretend that you're not my husband." I whisper. "Pretend that you're my best friend only. Or pretend you're in in love with me and

I don't know. I don't know, but just forget the us aspect of all of this and tell me what to do. Please."

He looks down at the soapy water and sighs slowly.

"Micah can't live with your Mom." he says finally. "Under no circumstance can he end up with her."

He takes a deep breath.

"So what do I do? I need to find a way to keep Micah safe and keep us safe." I gesture between he and I and my belly.

"Your nipples got darker." He says suddenly, reaching forward to lift one of my breasts up.

I swat at his hand.

"Danny, focus." I urge him.

He sighs.

"Grace, I invited Miley and Kyle over tonight so I can talk them into adopting Micah."

I hesitate.

"What?"

About a year ago in October, Miley went to the doctor to check her fertility and found out she can't have children at all. They were both devastated and agreed they would adopt eventually, but they haven't mentioned it since.

"I love Micah sweetheart, but he's not my son. I want to raise our children, and I know you feel the same way."

"Yeah."

"If we have to, we'll keep him, but if we can find a family that wants a child...like Kyle and Miley, we're in luck."

"Okay, but if one of my parents wins the custody battle, neither one of them are going to give Micah to Kyle and Miley."

"That's why neither one of them can win." He says.

"So what's your plan?" I ask.

He sighs. "My plan is simple." He says. "You crash the trial."

*****

I love Danny so much idk

Also, I'm thinking about a book four...unless you guys think that's too much~Sam

Chapter Seven: Doctor

A lot of you have been complaining because I cut off the honeymoon so part of this (in the beginning) is rated R

*****

Chapter Seven: Doctor

"You crash the trial." My husband says calmly.

I hesitate.

"What?"

"You walk into the trial in a tight dress accentuating your baby bump and completely interrupt, beg the judge to listen to you, and then throw all of lawyers off course. You make up their minds."

I stare at him.

"That's brilliant." I say.

"Right?"

"That way, Micah can go somewhere safe but close by so you can still have a relationship with him. He can still see your Dad but he gets raised as Kyle and Miley's son. They get a kid. We all win."

"What if Kyle and Miley want a baby?"

"Then we find another family. We will find somebody, and if we don't, he stays with us. Either way, Micah stays safe and so does our baby." He reaches under the water to put his hand on my belly.

"Danny, I don't know..." I trail off. "It's a good idea but it's risky."

"On the day of the trial, do you know who I want to see?" He asks.

"Who?"

"I want to see my sassy best friend that walked up to the front of English class and told everyone I broke her heart. I want that word strength. I want to feel every single word."

I nod slowly.

"So you want a savage."

He laughs.

"Yeah baby, I want a savage."

"Fine. I'm going to do it. Wanna know why?"

"Why?" He smiles.

"My Momma ain't raise no bitch."

He starts laughing.

"Oh god, I love you."

"I love you too." I smile.

He leans forward and kisses me softly, pulling me into his lap.

I kiss him back and after a moment, I can feel something pressing against me down there. I shift slightly so I don't accidentally slip on top of him, and then he starts to kiss down my jaw.

"You know one of us is going to die if we have sex in this tub, right?" I mumble breathlessly.

"I think we're going to be fine." He murmurs against my neck, sucking on my favorite spot.

Usually that just feels good but today it feels incredible. I feel his hands grasping my breasts and they've been so sensitive lately that it feels a million times better than it usually would. I tangle my fingers in his hair and tilt my head to the side to give him better access on my neck.

He presses his lips back to mine and reaches under the water to grab my hips, positioning me over top of him. I start to kiss down his jaw.

"Grace?" He mumbles.

"Hmm?" I hum, kissing his neck.

"I love you."

"I love you too." I murmur. I feel him positioning himself until his tip is pressed against me, and I sink myself on top of him.

*****

I sit in the doctors office, my leg bouncing up and down repeatedly. My husband sits next to me flipping through some pregnancy magazine.

"They should put some sports magazine in here for the fathers." Danny grumbles, tossing the magazine on the coffee table in the waiting room.

"Amen to that." A man nearby mutters. A women with brown hair sits next to him, but she doesn't look any more pregnant than I am. I see her smile a little bit and shake her head.

Danny glances at them and then leans close to me and whispers.

"Do you know what I just realized?"

Now, my husband is a very sweet man, but there are a few select people in the world, and we all know them, that can't whisper for shit. They're basically whisper shouting, and Danny has been that way since birth. If he was whispering to me from across the room, I could hear him.

"What?" I ask, glancing around the waiting room. It's two women are here alone, one with a ring and one without. Another woman has another lady with her. There is a teenage girl who is very pregnant and her Mom with her, and a teenage boy, and another woman who looks to be the boys mother. On top of that, there is four other couples, not including the one that just agreed with my husband and Danny and I. Two of those couples have kids with them, one looking to be Micah's age and the other is in diapers.

That makes up for twenty two people, not including the three people at the desk.

"Every single person in this room has had sex." Danny whispers loudly.

All twenty four heads turn, mine included, to look at him, but he remains oblivious.

"Mommy, what's sex?" The boy that looks to be Micah's age asks.

Danny's head snaps towards the child and back to me.

"Did I say that too loudly?" He whispers loudly.

"You can't whisper." I say, patting his hand. I look at the parents of the child. "I'm so sorry. My husband never learned how to whisper."

"It's completely fine." The mother laughs awkwardly and starts talking quietly to her child.

Danny looks like he wants to say something and then he presses his lips together and pulls out his phone.

A moment later, my screen lights up.

Hubby: I know how to whisper

Me: no you don't

Hubby: yes I do

Me: in second grade when we were in class we were talking crap about the teacher by passing notes and you whispered my name even though you sat next to me and the teacher heard you. She was in the joined classroom next door talking to the other teacher

I send it and watch him read it and he scowls at the screen.

Hubby: everyone has flaws. You married me anyways

Me: I love you baby, you know that

Hubby: I know. I love you too

I lock my screen.

"Gracelyn?"

Danny and I both look up at towards the voice. A nurse stands in the waiting room with pink scrubs. I stand up in sync with my husband and grab my purse, following him. My hand finds his because this isn't just some checkup. This is our first baby appointment. It's a big deal.

The nurse weighs me and then hands me a cup and a paper bag.

"We're going to have you take another pregnancy test just to be sure. This is your room right here." She points to a door with the number two above it. "We're going to be waiting in there."

I hand Danny my purse and phone and walk down the hall to the bathroom.

I do my business and wash my hands and clean off the cup, and then wash my hands again and head back down the hall into the room. The nurse takes the bag and sets it on the counter and she takes my blood pressure and listens to my heart.

"Everything looks good so far. The doctor will be in soon."

"Thank you." Danny says.

"Of course."

She walks out and shuts the door.

I sit down on the medical chair and wait.

"When are we telling my parents?" He asks. "I don't like that your Dad knows and mine doesn't."

"I don't like it either." I say. "Let's tell them on Christmas."

"You have morning sickness." He reminds me. "It's going to be hard to explain why you're throwing up throughout the day and sleeping so much."

"I'm sorry. I get so tired." I say.

"You have nothing to apologize for." He says.

I open my mouth to suggest we well them earlier, but there's a knock on the door and then the doctor walks in.

"Hi Mom and Dad." She smiles, sitting down on the stool. She rolls forward to shake both of our hands and turns to me. "How are you feeling today?"

"Tired." I say truthfully.

"That's to be expected." She smiles. She puts some gloves on a grabs a strip test from the drawer, grabbing the cup of my pee.

She unscrews the cap and dips the test into it, holding it for a few seconds. She lies it on the counter and turns around.

"So were you guys trying?" She asks.

"Yes. We were trying for about eight months." I nod.

"Okay, excellent. And when did you test positive?"

"Saturday morning." I say.

"Have you taken more than one test?"

"Yeah, we got a positive and then took three more." Danny says. "All of them were positive."

"Excellent." She says. She looks down at the test on the counter. "Great, make that five." She holds up the positive test and then throws it into the trash. She changes her gloves and rolls over to me.

"Now, do you know when your last period was?"

My last period, or my last missed period?"

"Your last period."

"Um...some time in September. I thought this goes by my last missed period."

"We go by your last actual period."

I rub my forehead, thinking back to September.

"It was around the fifteenth."

"Alright." She says. "So September fifteenth."

She looks like she's thinking. "So you're probably around thirteen weeks pregnant, but let's go ahead and do an ultrasound to make sure."

She reaches for the machine and I roll up my shirt.

I'm already thirteen weeks along? How is that? I thought I was only eight weeks, but I'm a month and one week later than I realized.

The doctor pours the gel on my belly and grabs the wand, turning on the machine.

I grab Danny's hand and I'm freaking out.

I'm thirteen weeks? How did I not know? That's already three months along! And I was spotting in October! Why I was I spotting?!

But I hear a warping sound on the monitor and my eyes lock on the screen, and all my worries vanish.

The baby is definitely bigger than eight weeks, and it's so clearly a baby.

"That's the heartbeat." The doctor smiles. I look at Danny and let out a little laugh. He kisses my cheek and keeps looking at the monitor. "Now this is the head, the body, the arms, knees, legs..." she trails off, moving the wand. The mutes the heartbeat sound. "Baby looks healthy." She smiles.

"And you're definitely thirteen weeks down to the day." She says. "I'm going to set your due date as June twenty fourth."

"I have been reading a lot of articles about when people found out the sex." Danny says. "And some woman found out at twelve weeks. Do you think it's a possibility we can find out today?"

"We can certainly try. Do you guys want to know?"

I look at Danny and he starts nodding.

"Yes." I tell the doctor, wiping the tears off my cheeks.

"Well let's try." She says.

She starts moving the wand around carefully and we all watch the screen. She positions the want between the baby's legs so we can see, moving it around.

After almost a minute of her moving the wand, she pauses the picture.

"That," she points to the spot between our babies legs. "Is a vagina."

Danny stands cheering and I start laughing with happiness. This is a miracle.

"Everything looks normal." She smiles.

"How sure are you though?" Danny asks.

She looks between my husband and I.

"I'm so sure that if I'm wrong, I will personally come to your house and paint the nursery blue."

We start laughing again.

"Do you want pictures?" She asks.

"Yes, lots and lots of pictures." I nod.

She prints out pictures and cleans off my belly. I pull my shirt down.

"Now, as far as you know, are there any health problems in your family histories?"

I look at Danny.

"Not as far as I know." I shake my head.

"Yeah, I don't think so." Danny says.

"Have you ever had surgery before?" She asks me.

"No." I shake my head.

"She had her tonsils removed when she was six." Danny says.

"Yeah, there was that."

"Okay, have you ever been pregnant before?"

"No." I smile, shaking my head.

A girl. We're having a girl.

"Okay, now I am going to need to take some blood so I can check and make sure there isn't anything wrong that needs to be monitored. We're also going to test your urine."

"Okay." I say.

"Give me one second." She holds up a finger and walks out, leaving me alone with Danny.

"We're having a girl!" He whispers. "Oh my god, I've never been more excited in my entire life."

He leans down and starts kissing my belly, causing me to laugh.

The doctor comes back with the stuff to take my blood. She goes on the side of my chair Danny isn't on and hands me a stress ball.

"Are you a smoker or taking tobacco?" She asks me.

"No."

"Do you drink alcohol?"

"Nope." I shake my head.

"Excellent. Are you on any medications?"

"Nope." I smile.

"Alright, that's wonderful. Now if you get headaches, Tylenol is the safest thing for you to take."

"Okay." I nod.

"Have you gotten prenatal vitamins yet?" She asks.

"No I have not." I say as she ties the rubber band around my arm.

"Okay, I recommend RainbowLight. It's all natural. The only con is that it's expensive, but your health insurance might cover it."

"Can you text me that?" I ask Danny.

"Sure." He nods. He grabs his phone and starts typing. She pushes on a vein in my arm and I squeeze the ball to help her.

After a moment, she inserts the needle.

Most people hate needles but I don't mind them.

I watch my blood fill the small container and then she takes the needle out and tapes a cotton ball where the needle was.

She grabs my cup of pee and the blood tube, walking out of the room.

She comes back and collects everything she used to take my blood, and then she sits down again.

"Now what symptoms have you been having?" She asks.

"Um, sore breasts and nausea, but the nausea was for about three days and then it stopped, which was weird."

"Everyone is different." She says with a shrug. "You're lucky you're not one of the Mom's that gets all the symptoms."

I laugh easily.

"Now do you guys have any questions for me?"

"I had spotting back in October. Does that matter?"

"Well your baby girl looks healthy. It's normal to have some spotting around the time of implantation, and that was probably in October." She says.

"Is sex safe?" I ask.

"Sex is fine as long as you're not uncomfortable." She says.

"Can I call you with questions?" I ask, glancing at her name tag.

Dr. Marie Edwards

"Yes, here is my number." She grabs a business card and hands it to me. "If you can't get ahold of me, leave a message. If it's serious, call 911 and then call me. You can text me, too."

"Thank you." I say.

"You're welcome. Any more questions?"

She looks between Danny and I.

"Can she travel safely?"

"The safest time to travel is between eighteen and twenty four weeks." She says.

"What's the best advice you can give her?" Danny asks.

"Just listen to your body." She says to both of us. "If you feel like you need to stop what you're doing, stop. If you want to eat something, it might not be the food, but whats in the food."

"Okay." Danny hesitates. "How much weight should she be gaining?"

"Anywhere between twenty five and thirty five pounds." She says.

"Okay." Danny says. "Can you think of anything else?" His hands rest on my left arm.

"No, I think that's it." I smile.

"Alright, well your next appointment will be at sixteen weeks, so go ahead and schedule that, and don't forget to get your prenatal vitamins."

"Thank you." Danny says. She hands him the pictures of our daughter and he walks me to the desk to schedule the next appointment.

It's December twentieth, so we make it for January tenth. We pay the copay for the appointment today, and then Danny walks me outside.

"I can't believe it Gracie." He says the second we're alone. "We're having a baby girl!"

"I know." I grin. "I'm so excited."

"This is incredible. I'm so happy."

"Me too." I smile.

He walks with me to the Jeep and takes the keys.

"Let's go to Target and get the vitamins." He says as he opens the passenger door for me

I look at the time on my phone.

"Actually, we have to go pick Micah up from school." I tell him as I get in the car. "And then we can get the vitamins."

"Okay, let's go."

*****

That's right. A girl

~Sam

Chapter Eight: News

"Lauren." I suggest.

"No. Rachel?"

"No." I shake my head.

"Quinn?" He asks.

"No. Amber?"

"Nope." He says. "What about Julia?"

"No. Juliette?"

He hesitates. "That's cute but I think that should be the middle name."

I hesitate, shifting my head on his side.

"Juliette." I repeat. "Alright. Do you want to spell it J-U-I-L-E-T or J-U-I-L-E-T-T-E?"

"J-U-I-L-E-T." He says.

"Alright." I nod, circling the name in the magazine. "What about Marissa?"

"No." He says. "Opal?"

"Eh. No."

"Okay." He sighs. "Mariposa?"

I open my mouth to say no and then I close it.

"Mariposa." I repeat slowly. "We can call her Posie."

"That's cute, right? I think we should name her Mariposa."

"Mariposa Juliet Grey." I mumble. "Danny, that's the name."

"You think so?" He asks.

"I do. Posie."

He sits up excitedly and rolls over, kissing my belly.

"You know, when you lay down I can kinda see a bump." He tells me.

"Really?" I ask.

"Yeah." He nods. He puts both hands on my belly. "Hi little one, it's Daddy." He murmurs. "I know you can't hear me yet but Mama and I decided we're going to call you Mariposa. Did you know Mariposa means butterfly?"

My stomach growls and Danny asks.

"She kicked!" He exclaims.

"Babe, that was my stomach."

His smile falls.

"Well stop it, this is between me and my daughter."

I swat at him and he smiles, kissing my belly and then moving to kiss my lips.

I hear the doorbell ring and then the front door shuts, causing both of us to get up and walk to the balcony. Caleb and Beatrice left yesterday to get here before Christmas and I see them in the living room.

Danny takes my hand and we go downstairs together.

"Hey guys." He says. We exchange hugs. "How's it going? How was the drive?

"It was alright." Caleb smiles, but he looks tired.

"Where's Micah?" Beatrice wonders.

"He's at school." I say, bouncing with excitement.

I want to blurt the news.

"Can you guys help us move everything in the truck into our storage unit?" Caleb asks.

"Yeah okay, we need to talk to you guys though." Danny says, completely disregarding what his Dad just said.

He walks to the kitchen.

We wrapped a gift with our little secret inside.

"Okay, but can it wait?" Beatrice asks. "We just drove eight hours. I had to tow my car behind Dad's truck and he had to drive a giant U-Haul."

"Mom, it can't wait." Danny says.

She sighs.

"Alright, fine." She sighs.

"Sit down." He points to the table.

They both sit down at the table and I get the wrapped box. Danny sets the camera up to record and I hand them the box.

"Open it together."

"Christmas is in a couple days." Beatrice says.

"So?" I ask. "Open it!"

Caleb gestures for Beatrice to open it and Danny puts both hands on my shoulders while we wait.

She rips the paper off and looks at the simple shoebox. We wrapped the lid and the box so that it would look cute. She pushes it towards Caleb and he flips it open.

On the lid are the words:

Roses are red, violets are blue. We have a secret, and here's your clue!

There's tissue paper covering the contents of the box. Beatrice looks more alert now, pulling the tissue paper off the top.

In the box sits two tan little baby booties, causing Beatrice to shriek.

"You're pregnant?!" She exclaims, her eyes filling with tears. We both start laughing and I nod.

"Yeah. I'm thirteen weeks and two days."

"And we already know the sex. The doctor said she's so sure that if she's wrong, she'll come paint the nursery herself."

"This is great news!" Caleb exclaims, standing up from the table. "I'm going to be a Grandpa!"

They start hugging us.

"So what is it?!" Caleb asks. "A boy or a girl?"

"It's a girl." I say, beaming.

"Oh my god, a granddaughter!" Beatrice hugs both of us again.

"We've already picked a name, too." Danny laughs. "Mariposa, but we're going to call her Posie. Her middle name is Juliet."

"Mariposa Juliet Grey. That's beautiful." Caleb smiles.

Beatrice pushes me down into the chair.

"So how are you feeling? When did you find out? Are you taking prenatal vitamins? You really need to listen to your body."

I laugh.

"I'm okay, I'm just tired a lot. I'm taking RainbowLight, which takes like metal. Danny thinks it's the iron in the pills."

"It probably is." She nods. "So you're already in your second trimester. Are you nervous? Scared?"

"Both." I say.

She turns to her son. "And what about you?"

"I'm good, Mom."

"When did you guys find out?" Caleb asks. "Were you trying?"

"We found out actually on Saturday. When we disappeared after being questioned, we took a test and it was positive."

"Oh wow, you found out late." Beatrice says.

"I know." I shrug. "But the doctor said everything is normal. She did a urine test and a blood test and they were good."

"We've been trying since April but it wasn't working..." Danny trails off.

"I was getting more upset every time we got a negative and then Micah came and we agreed to stop trying, and the next day I tested positive."

"That's great." Beatrice smiles. "So who else knows?"

I clear my throat.

This is the part of the conversation I was not looking forward to.

"My grandparents." I say. "And...my Dad."

Silence.

"You told your Dad?" Caleb asks slowly.

"Scott showed up after everyone left on Saturday night and tried to get us to give him Micah because Eileen buried the legal files on Grace's custody case. He said he thought Eileen was going to win and he was going to take Micah and move to another country."

Beatrice snorts.

"I told him that he can't because I'm pregnant and if the cops come here questioning and I have to lie and they find out after the baby is born-"

"They will throw both of you in jail and take the baby." Caleb says.

"Right. We were going to tell you guys first." I say, reaching across the table to grab one of their hands. "I swear, but you know my Dad."

Caleb pats my hands and nods.

"It's not your fault. So what is he planning to do to protect Micah from Eileen?" He asks.

"I'm crashing the trail."

Both of them raise their eyebrows.

"What?" Beatrice asks.

"I'm crashing the trial." I repeat.

"You're crashing the trial?" Caleb asks slowly. "When is the trial?"

"April twenty eighth."

"And when is your due date?" Beatrice asks.

"June twenty first." I reply.

"Grace, you're going to be seven months pregnant by then." Beatrice whispers.

"No, I don't think this is a good idea." Caleb says as he shakes his head. "That's way too much stress for you and the baby."

"Well we don't really have another choice, Dad." Danny says quietly. "If she doesn't go, Micah lives with Eileen."

"That's not happening." I say immediately. "If that happens, I will take him to another country myself."

Everyone is quiet and I know they know I'm serious.

"Fine, but we're coming with you." Beatrice says.

"We need you here to take care of Micah." Danny says.

"Micah can go to your Grandparents house." Beatrice says. "Caleb and I are coming."

"And what if she goes into labor?" Danny asks. "You guys are planning to ride all the way back to North Carolina stuck between a car seat.

"Yes." Caleb says.

The four of us kind of have this stare down.

"Either that or we follow behind you."

I rub my forehead and sigh.

"Alright, fine." I say.

"If Elizabeth and Matthew can't watch Micah, you guys are staying." Danny says seriously.

"Deal." Caleb replies.

*****

Sorry this was shorter that normal~Sam

Chapter Nine: Christmas

Chapter Nine: Christmas

Everyone is sitting around the living room. Our family on my Dad's side and Danny's Dad's side and part of his Mom's are sitting around the house. Miley and Kyle are here and they have a few of their relatives too. The more people, the better. It's just homey and exciting having everyone around.

It's snowing, which I think is awesome because it's Christmas. We told the whole family about the baby and everyone is really excited and they keep asking us questions. We already opened the gifts and Danny and I bought a lot of stuff for Micah from Santa and he told us he only gets a few things a year and I know for a fact they're from my Dad only.

The doorbell rings and Danny starts to get up, but I'm right by the door.

See, at our house there really isn't any hiding the front door from the living room, because everyone can see the door from the living room because there aren't any walls blocking it.

I walk over to the door and pull it open, expecting, or hoping, to see a neighbor with a plate of cookies.

But it's not cookies, it's my Dad.

Oh god, this is not a good day to show up here.

Since I only opened the door I crack, I grab Danny's coat off the railing next to the door and slip outside, shutting the door behind me. I put the coat on.

"Dad, it's really not a good day to show up here." I whisper. "Your entire side of the family is here, Danny's family is here, Caleb and Beatrice are here."

He looks like he wants to come inside and be included.

"I'm going back to Florida today." He stuffs his hands in his pockets. "And I hate to do this, but you have to let me take Micah. Eileen can't get custody."

"Dad, no." I say. "I have a plan."

"I understand Grace, but if there's a risk to your plan, there's a risk to Micah's safety. I know you think I'm a horrible person, but I didn't know she was giving him alcohol. She hit him once when I was in the bathroom, and I protected him from her. I didn't know she was giving him alcohol, and the deal was that if she made dinner, I cleaned up while she gave him a bath. I heard the water running every night-"

"You told me when I called you after Micah got here that you didn't know if he had eaten and you didn't know when the last time he had a bath was."

"Because I dropped him off at the airport in the morning." He says seriously. "And the bath thing-I literally found out the night before when I tucked him into bed that he never gets baths because he told me, Grace, I swear."

"And what's this about him not having a bedroom? What happened to my old room?"

"Eileen turned that half of the house into her 'girl cave' and every time I tried to go over there, she yelled at me. I'm not kidding. That half of the house was forbidden."

I shiver violently and then I sigh

"I promised you that I would fix things, and I will, but I can't think straight while Micah is at risk."

"If you take Micah, you could put me at risk."

"No Grace, if I take Micah and the cops show up, you tell them the truth. Tell them I threatened you with a gun to keep you quiet. I don't care, but you do what you have to to protect your family and I'll do what I have to to protect mine."

I stuff my hands in the pockets of Danny's jacket.

"Dad, you're not taking him." I say. "And there are a lot of people in my house right now that you will have to fight to get to him."

"Grace." He pleads. "If I take him now, You stay safe, the baby stays safe, Micah stays safe."

"No." I say. "Will you please just listen to me for once? I know I'm your kid but I'm twenty six years old. I know what I'm doing."

"I know that, but-"

"Just trust me." I say. "Please."

"I want to know your plan." He says.

"Dad-"

"Grace, at least tell me the plan."

Another gust of wind makes it's way onto the porch and I shiver.

"Let's go inside." He says.

"Dad, there are people in this house that haven't seen you-"

"I don't care, alright? I can handle whatever they have to say."

"I'm sure you can." I say. "But it's just risky."

"Well-"

I hear the front door opening behind me and my husband stands there. He opened the door all the way, which means everyone can see my Dad.

Danny's eyebrows rise slightly and the he steps aside.

"Come inside. It's cold." He says.

Dad looks at me and I sigh, going back into the house. I shed Danny's coat and put it back on the railing. Dad steps into the house and Danny shuts the door.

All the laughter is gone from the air and everyone is just...quiet.

"Scott." Uncle Jerry says to his brother.

"Jerry." Dad replies.

"What are you doing here?" Aunt Denise asks. She's the youngest of the three.

"It's fine." I say. "He was here a few days ago."

"He left a few days ago." Grandma says. "Why are you back?"

I look at Dad.

"You drove all the way back here?" I whisper.

"Yes."

Micah comes into the living room from the bathroom. He has a toy in his hand and his eyes land on Dad.

"Hi Dad." He says.

"Hey bud."

Danny moves behind me and I feel his hands on my shoulders, something I've noticed he has been doing since we found out about the baby. He does it every time I'm in a situation that could stress me out.

Dad looks at me. "Why don't we ask him what he wants?" He suggests.

"He's five." I whisper.

"So?"

Dad walks over to Micah and crouches down.

"What do you say that you and I leave?" He asks.

Micah hesitates.

"And go where?"

"Somewhere far away from here, where Mom can't hurt you."

He looks down, his eyebrows furrowing.

"Can Grace and Danny come?" He asks. "Grace is having a baby, you know." He smiles. "I'm going to be an Uncle."

Dad looks down at his hands, nodding.

"Yeah, but no bud, they can't come with us. But it'll be fun."

"I don't want to go." Micah says.

"But-"

"I want to stay here. Danny and Grace take care of me. I have my own bed here. I get to take a bath whenever I want to. Why can't I stay here? Mom isn't here."

Dad sighs and stands up, and he looks frustrated.

"Listen," he says to me. "If you fuck up, I swear to God-"

"Let me be clear." I cut him off. "If I fuck up, it won't be my fault. It will be your fault. You knew exactly what you were doing. I told you this was going to happen, but I will always be your teenage daughter that knows nothing."

"Grace, would you stop bringing that up? This has nothing to do with that, this has to do with your mother and your little brother."

"I'm well aware what this has to do with." I snap.

He sighs, running his hands across his face.

"I need money."

Silence. The house is so quiet, you can hear a pin drop.

"That's the truth. I sent Micah to you because I knew you could take care of him, but I drove out here because I needed money, but I didn't want to ask you, but I came back because I need money. I can't pay the lawyer, I'm going to lose my apartment, and you clearly have money." He gestures around Danny and I's house. "I need help. After this mess is over, I will fix things, but until then-"

I tune him out because all I can think about is the little baby growing inside of me.

I don't want her coming into this world like this.

"-and I love you kid, and I'm going to fix things, but I need money."

I can feel the heat radiating off of my husbands body. His of his hands are on my shoulder and his touch is gentle but I know he's pissed.

"Since I was fourteen, I have been wondering what my point was in this world." I say, cutting him off. "I tried to kill myself when I was sixteen, and you want to know why I didn't?"

He sighs.

"Why?"

"Because of Danny."

He stays silent.

"You knew how bad Mom was and you subjected me to that torture. You should have gotten me out of that house the second you saw her raise her hand to me."

"There was nowhere for you to go." He says.

"Bullshit!" I snarl. "I'm sure almost every person in this house would have opened their door to me, and you knew that! It took her trying to kill me for you to act, and then you were good for a while but you were careless, and you promised me you wouldn't go back, but you did. You blamed me for the abuse she did to me, and I have spent years waking up with nightmares, and when we were in Maryland and I woke up screaming, you'd didn't come in to make sure I was okay. Maybe it was guilt. Who knows. But Danny has been there every single time I have needed him. At seventeen years old, he was more of a man than you were at thirty five. Then you swoop in and blame me for her abuse, for the issues you let happen! I cut you off, and I came back because I miss you, and dammit, Danny told me it was a bad idea, and he was right, because you told me you were going to find me and fix things. Then I open my door and a five year old is standing on my porch in freezing weather in a t-shirt and shorts, and you promise me this isn't how you're fixing things, and then you have the nerve to show up here after all the damage you let happen to me, and you have the nerve to ask for money?"

"Grace-"

"I'm talking." I snap. He presses his lips together and stays silent. "My husband was there when you weren't. He could ask me for anything in the world and I would die trying to give it to him." I pause. "After blaming me and letting me be abused, I shut you out. Now I made something of myself and you want to come swooping back into my life? You weren't there to walk me down the aisle. You weren't at my college graduation. You weren't there. Now you're here, on Christmas, but you're here because I have something you need! My child will never deal with this shit. My child will be loved and cherished. My child will never have to wonder what her worth is. I will never treat my baby the way you and Mom have treated Micah and I." I take a deep breath. "Micah is staying with me. I will protect him, but I swear to God if you don't leave my property, I'm going to call the police and have you arrested."

"Gracelyn," Dad begins.

Danny removes his hands from my shoulder and I hear the front door open.

"Get out."

Dad looks back at Micah.

"You can't keep him. I gave him to you. You can't keep him."

I walk across the house and push Micah behind my back.

Beatrice gets up from the couch and moves to stand in front of me, and then Abby moves in front of her and Megan moves in front of her, and then Brecklyn, and Christian and Jackson and Aunt Vickie and Uncle Jerry and Caleb, until everyone in the room is completely surrounding me and Micah from my Dad.

A couple of seconds later, the front door shuts.

Everyone disperses.

Money. He wanted money.

I thought he wanted me for once in his life.

And the worst part about all of this?

I'm not surprised in the slightest.

*****

I'm sad and hungry and in a really bad mood today

~Sam

Chapter Ten: Shopping

Chapter Ten: Shopping

I really didn't want to cry but I ended up going upstairs and crying anyways, and I was mad because my Dad put stress on the baby, and I was mad because I cried.

Now I'm sitting on the couch in Danny and I's sitting room in our bedroom, watching the snow fall out the window. I took the blanket off our bed and wrapped my body in it.

Danny came up here four times and I sent him away, so he sent Abby and I sent her away too, and both of my grandparents have come up here, Beatrice came up here...but I told them to get out.

They've left me alone for a while, and then I hear knocking on the bedroom door.

I don't respond, but after a second the door opens and closes and I hear footsteps on the carpet.

Caleb sits down next to me on the couch.

"Just-"

"I'm not leaving." He says, looking at me. "I'm going to sit here with you in silence."

I open my mouth to protest but he just grabs the other end of the blanket and pulls it over his lap.

I don't say a word to him and he doesn't say anything to me, but it makes me feel better to know I'm not sitting here alone, so I ask the one question I can't get out of my head.

"Do you think I'm going to turn out like my parents?"

He looks at me and hesitates.

"You already haven't."

I look down at my hands.

"I probably have you and Beatrice to thank for that. You guys are more parents to me than mine have been in a long time."

He sighs.

"I just wish my Dad didn't come over today. I don't want to be sad. I want to focus on the baby and Danny. This day should be happy. It's Christmas."

"Grace, the only reason this day isn't happy is because you're in here alone. I know you're upset but at least go downstairs and pretend to be happy."

I look at my father-in-law.

"I'm done, Caleb. I'm done trying with him. Danny and I, we don't need this. Our daughter does need this. I'm done trying to have parents. I don't need them. I'm happier without them. I'll protect Micah by keeping him away from my parents, and I'll protect my daughter by giving up on my parents. There's no point. They don't care."

He's quiet and I wait for him to say something.

"I'm sorry." He says finally.

"It's not your fault." I say, standing up. "Let's go downstairs."

He stands up and I grab the comforter and throw it on the bed, walking out of the bedroom and down the stairs.

*****

"I never thought this would happen to me." I mutter, scrolling through my laptop.

Miley and Megan laugh and Abby rolls her eyes.

On my screen is a website that sells bras, because I went from at 32D to a 34F.

That's right. A 34F.

My breasts are enormous and they're so sensitive. My nipples burn when something rubs against them.

It's only been four weeks but my body has been changing rapidly. My jeans are too tight so I had to get maternity clothes. My shirts are too tight because my breasts are large, and I have a little tiny bump. To a blind eye, you can't tell I'm pregnant, but somebody that knows me knows I'm pregnant.

It's late January and life is just normal. Caleb and Beatrice are out looking for a house. Micah is being a good kid and he's gained ten pounds and now he looks healthy. He bathes every other day unless he asks to take a bath early. His bedtime is eight o'clock, and this weekend is his sixth birthday. He and Danny play video games and I help him with his homework, and every weekend if there is snow on the ground, Danny takes him west in North Carolina and they go sledding.

They're out today and Kyle went with them.

Megan moved to North Carolina and she bought a house. Her parents and brothers went back to Michigan, but I know Jackson and Christian are thinking about moving down here and getting a house together.

"Grace, can I ask you something?" Miley asks.

"Sure." I say, grabbing my wallet to get my debit card.

"Are you going to tell the judge to give custody to your Dad?"

"Absolutely not." I say.

"So what are you doing with Micah?"

"We're keeping him." I say. Danny and I discussed it and we don't want to just pawn Micah off to somebody. We'll keep him.

"Yeah, but what if like...somebody else wanted to raise him?" She asks quietly.

I raise my eyes from my wallet to Miley.

"Somebody else like who?" I ask quietly.

"Well, like me and Kyle."

Everyone is kind of quiet.

"Because I can't have kids..." she trails off. "And you are having one." She gestures to my body. "And Micah is a good kid, and...well he seems to like Kyle and I. We wouldn't hurt him like your parents did."

Danny was originally going to ask them to take him anyways.

"How long have you been thinking about this?" I ask her.

"Well I..." she sighs. "Since Christmas."

A month. She's been thinking about this for a month.

"And Kyle..."

"Kyle was the one who brought it up." She says softly. "You can see him whenever you want obviously, spend holidays with him..." she trails off, and she looks nervous to even bring the subject up.

But I don't know. It's hard for me to trust people with Micah.

"Well it's obviously an option..." I trail off. "But I don't know."

"Well will you think about it?" She asks.

"Yeah, I'll think about it."

"Thank you." She says.

"You're welcome."

I type in my credit card information to buy the bras.

I don't want Micah to feel like we just pawned him off on Miley and Kyle, but they really want him and Micah deserves parents.

If I could be raised by good parents or my big sister, I would pick good parents.

But is five years old too old to switch parents? Will Micah ever consider Kyle and Miley his parents?

*****

This is a horrible day.

This morning Danny was out looking at a house with Beatrice and Caleb and Micah got a stain on a white shirt. I started filling up the sink in the laundry room so I could soak his shirt to get the stain out, and then forgot about it.

I remembered forty five minutes later when there was water coming out from under the door.

I used all the towels to clean up the floor and then I washed them and put Micah's shirt in the sink. I took a nap with Pepper on the couch and then Danny, Caleb, and Beatrice came to pick me up for lunch. They asked me if I had enough energy to go with them to look at houses today and I said yes.

I didn't want to go but Danny gently explained to me that he knows how to do the work, but he doesn't know what work to do if I'm not there.

And I'm in my second trimester, so I can be up doing things. I'm still only seventeen weeks, but I feel like I'm forty weeks.

The moment Danny pulls into the driveway, Caleb starts complaining.

"There's no garage."

"Let's go look at it." Danny says calmly.

We all get out and walk up to the door. The realtor texted Beatrice and said he was here, so I ring the bell

After a minute, the door opens.

The first thing that comes into my mind is one word.

Narrow.

It's basically a long wide hallway for the living room. To the left is a hall with four door. Three are bedrooms and one is a small bathroom. To the right is a dining room that really isn't a dining room, and on the other side of the dining room is the kitchen.

The biggest bedroom is supposed to be the master but it's so narrow and the master bath is hardly a bathroom.

There is a door that leads into a garage, but there isn't a garage door outside.

There needs to be a lot of changes.

"How much did you say this house was?" I ask the man.

"Two hundred thousand." He says.

Okay, their price limit is three hundred thousand. We could definitely fix the house up.

The kitchen itself is a U shape and it's narrow, but there really isn't any fixing it.

I guess the realtor has been showing them a ton of houses and they were talking about me, so he knows what Danny and I do for a living.

Everyone just looks at me expectantly.

"It's just so narrow." I say. "We need to cut into the house to put a two car garage door, which is a few thousand dollars. The master isn't really a master, which means we have to take out a wall." I start walking across the house and they follow me. I point to the wall and turn to my husband.

"That's a load-bearing wall, which means we have to put in a beam, which is another couple thousand dollars."

"You want to join two of the bedrooms?" Beatrice asks.

"That's the only way to get a master, but I can't give you a master suite, unless we join the two bathrooms and the laundry room and morph them into one bathroom, but that means the entire house uses this one bathroom."

"But you can do it?" Caleb asks.

"We can do it." I stuff my hands in the pocket of my jacket.

"I don't like it." Beatrice says. "I don't see the grandbabies running around here."

"Mom, you're not buying a house for our children." Danny says.

"We're going to have sleepovers with them." She says. "I want them to grow up and know this is their grandparents house. I want it to look like their grandparents house, and it doesn't."

Everyone looks at me.

"I'm sorry. You just don't have the property space to get what you want."

"Alright, this isn't our house." Caleb says. "We want one that screams..."

"We want one that screams Grandma and Grandpa." Beatrice says.

*****

He took us to another house, but this one had only the master bedroom upstairs but the ceilings were low and vaulted so you hit your head, and it was choppy and the closet and small bathroom were across the hall. I could have worked with that house it it was expensive and Beatrice and Caleb hated it.

Now we're pulling up to a two story yellow house with brown shutters. It's two stories and has a porch going across the front of the house.

"This is it." Beatrice says. "It needs to be painted, but this is it."

The front yard is completely ripped up with patches of dirt where the driveway should be.

"There is no garage." Caleb says.

"It's detached." I point to the matching garage to the left of the house.

"Let's just give it some thought." Beatrice says, unbuckling her seatbelt.

The realtor is waiting out front.

"How much?" I ask him.

"This one is one seventy nine nine." He says.

Oh yeah, with their budget at three hundred thousand, we get can them done under budget.

The house is lifted and I would paint it. Danny takes my hand as I walk up the steps so I don't fall. The wood on the porch is sturdy and nice.

The floor is a beautiful oak floor. Right when you walk in is the staircase. To the right is a bedroom and a bathroom. To the left is a large living room but it's cut off from the rest of the house. The bedroom on the right has a walk in closet and on the other side of that wall is the kitchen. It's a good size, and the dining room is attached but it's actually big.

I just don't like how cut off everything is. It's all choppy.

There is a bathroom attached to the bedroom with an entrance in the hall as well.

I feel a plan formulating in my mind and everyone follows me upstairs.

Directly to the left is a large master bedroom and a master bathroom with only a shower.

In front of the stairs is a door to a bathroom.

To the right of the stairs is a door to another bedroom, and down the hall is another bedroom.

"I like it, but it's so choppy." Caleb says.

"Well it's way under budget and you have the space to work with it." I say. "The garage is theirs, right?" I point towards the part of the yard that has the garage.

"Actually, that isn't, but it's for sale."

"So we have to buy the house and the garage?" Caleb asks.

"Yes. The garage is only eleven thousand dollars."

"If they buy the garage, does that become part of their property? Like can they pave a driveway?"

"Yes." He says.

"Okay, so you're spending one eighty one. That's still over a hundred thousand under budget."

"So what's the plan?" Beatrice asks me.

I sigh and walk down the stairs. Everyone follows me.

"Alright, I want to take down the wall around the stairs and open it up. Put railings up the side, put a beam in this wall because it's load bearing." I put my hand on the wall to the left of the stairs. "The pantry right here comes out so everything is open. Then we move the pantry here." I put my hand on the wall next to the fridge. "Or we build a pantry around the refrigerator, but that an be a paint because then if the fridge breaks, you can't get whatever fridge you want because you have to follow dimensions." I take a second to breathe because I've been getting short of breath lately. It's only because my uterus is growing and pressing up against my diaphragm, which is the muscle below my lungs. "Either way, we will get you that pantry, or we can leave that one up, but it won't feel as open.

"Let's move the pantry." Beatrice says.

"If we get the house." Caleb reminds her.

"If we get the house." She repeats.

"How many bedrooms do you want?" I ask. "I would like to make this dining room the breakfast area, and then the downstairs bedroom the dining room."

They both exchange glances.

"That seems good." Beatrice says.

"Okay, great." I take a deep breath. "Now I want to turn this bathroom into a half bathroom and open up this closet so you can have a little area for wine.

"That's a good idea." Caleb says.

"Obviously we'll rework the kitchen, get new counters and cabinets. I imagine we would get cabinets that go up to the ceiling to give you that extra storage."

I head back up the stairs, taking my time to go up because I'd rather be slow than dart up the stairs and slip.

"Now I want to take the master bathroom and get a tub that is large like the one in ours." I put my hand on Danny's arm. "And then put a shower head in it. Other than that, I think the second floor is good aside from sanding the floors and refinishing them. Fresh paint...maybe some crown molding."

"This sounds good." Beatrice says. "I like the idea of opening up the staircase."

"Would you change the outside?" Caleb asks.

"I would repaint it for sure. Maybe a dark blue and a red door? Or we should put a fresh paint of yellow on it and repaint the shutters. I would put sod in the front where the grass is ripped up and if you buy the garage, I would paint it to match the house and pave the driveway...and put a better fence up instead of that chain one."

"Is all of this in the budget?" Beatrice asks.

"Yes, and then some." Danny says.

We all go back downstairs and Beatrice and Caleb go into the living room to talk.

After a few minutes, they come back.

"We decided-"

I stop listening though, because I feel something in my belly, like a little nudge, but it's from inside.

The baby. I just felt the baby.

It goes away after a moment, and then I feel it again, and I swear I can feel her little elbow against my abdomen.

After a second, she stills and I don't feel it again, but it's unlike anything I have ever felt before.

*****

I work so early all next week I am dreading it so much

~Sam

Chapter Eleven: April Twenty Eighth

This chapter is one of the longest ones I've written in a while

*****

Chapter Eleven: April Twenty Eighth

I slowly watched as things began to change.

Beatrice and Caleb bought a house and we knocked down walls and are working on renovating it. Micah got close with Kyle and Miley and now he asks me every single weekend to have sleepovers at their house. When I asked him why, he told me they read him bedtime stories and take him outside to play and help him with homework.

Obviously we do too, but he insisted it's different.

I watched as my belly grew larger and the baby began kicking more, until Danny would sit in bed with me at night and read our daughter stories, and she responds to his voice. I can feel her jump in my tummy from loud noises.

Now I'm twenty nine weeks pregnant down to the day, and it's April twenty eighth.

I left Micah in North Carolina. He was going to stay with my grandparents but he begged and pleaded to stay with Miley and Kyle.

I smooth out my dress, which is navy blue and skintight. My makeup is on and my hair is up in a sophisticated style.

Danny reaches over to take my hand and squeeze it, and I watch as we get closer to the courthouse.

I found out online that the trial is at 10:30AM.

It's eleven, so I'm a little anxious because we're late.

I keep my hands on my belly and watch as we get closer to the courthouse.

Danny pays for four hours.

Beatrice, Caleb, Danny and I walk over to the crosswalk. I waddle next to Danny and he keeps his hand on me at all times.

When the light changes for us to walk, we go across the street and I use the ramp instead of the stairs.

We walk into the door and go up to the second floor, where they make us go through security.

After we've all been cleared, I turn to one of the guards.

"Can you tell me where the Levinsky custody trial is?" I ask.

"Down that hall, third door on your right. It's a full house."

"Thank you." I say.

He nods and I stop to take a couple of deep breaths.

"Sweetheart, all you're doing is telling your story." Danny says softly. "You can do this."

This is all for my baby brother, so with a nod, I turn around and march down the hall, my heels clicking against the tile floor.

As far as Micah knows, we're on a business trip.

I stop outside the double doors, take a deep breath and throw them open.

They open loudly.

It's all about the entrance.

My Mother is at the stand being questioned, and the look on her face turns venomous when I walk in. Every single head in the court room turns, and I hear Danny, Caleb, and Beatrice enter silently behind me. The doors click shut and I clear my throat.

I wrote a whole speech for this and I have it in the pocket of my dress, but I can't read it.

The look of pure hatred on my Mom's face is enough to make me get chills.

The last time she gave me that look, her hands were locking around my throat.

"Your honor, I would like to say a few words." I say.

The judge looks completely shocked.

"We can't just take random people up to the stand." The judge says, annoyed.

"Your honor, I'm seven months pregnant and I drove down here from North Carolina to say what I have to say."

Dead silence, and then the judge nods slowly, eyeing my baby bump for a moment.

"Who are you?" She asks.

"My name is Gracelyn Beth Grey. My maiden name Gracelyn Beth Levinsky. I'm Scott and Eileen's first child."

The look on my Mom's lawyers face goes from confused to pissed, but Dad's lawyer doesn't look surprised in the slightest.

The judge eyes my mother and then my father.

"How come nobody knew you had another child?"

"Because we don't." Mom says. Her voice is full of hatred.

"I have my birth certificate to prove it, your honor." I say, taking a deep breath.

"Let me see." She says.

I pull my birth certificate from the manila folder in my hand and walk up the aisle. The officer takes it from me and makes me stand next to where my Dad is sitting.

The judge reads over my birth certificate and holds it out. The officer takes it and gives it back to me.

"Eileen, please return to your seat and let your daughter take the stand."

Nobody says a word as my Mom loudly rises from the stand and walks to her seat, glaring at me the entire time. I walk up to the stand and sit down.

"Whenever you're ready." The judge says.

I look at Danny in the crowd and take a deep breath.

"The man and woman that raised me tucked me into bed every night and read me a bedtime story. They would bake with me, taught me how to ride a bike, normal parent stuff." I clear my throat. "I was raised alongside my best friend, who is now my husband. When I was ten years old, my best friend moved to Daytona Beach, Florida."

The courthouse is in Daytona Beach.

"About a year after he moved, my Mom lost her job." I clear my throat. "And she was home all the time, which was fun at first, but the light I saw in her eyes slowly faded until it was gone." I take a deep breath. "I think I was in seventh grade when she first got drunk. I remember that night as thought it was yesterday. It was just a normal day, where I would go to school and come home. Back then I had one of those flip phones where you has to press numbers a few times to get certain letters." I pause. "And I was on the phone with my best friend who had moved and I was...twelve, I think. My Mom asked me to help with dishes and I told her I would after I finished my homework. Well I finished it and forgot because I was a kid, and kids forget. The woman that raised me was gentle and loving, but when my Mom saw me on the phone with my friend, my Dad was in the living room and my Mom walked in. She took the phone from my hand and raised her hand to hit me." I feel my throat tightening and I clear my throat. "My Dad yelled at her and grabbed her wrist before he could hit her. He told me to take my phone and go to my room, and I heard them screaming for the rest of that night. It wasn't until two in the morning that my Dad came into my room to give me my dinner. That was the first time anybody that loved me tried to hurt me." I look down at the stand and will myself to just get through this. "It kept happening like that over the next...oh, four years? I would do something every kid does and she would try to hurt me. She never did because my Dad was there and I stayed away from her if he wasn't home." I take a deep breath. "I remained friends with my best friend through the years, and his parents were like my second parents." I pause. "One day in the beginning of my junior year in high school, I came home after school to my Mom passed out. My Dad was in the kitchen and I knocked a pan off the counter and woke my Mom up, and she tried to hit me, my Dad stopped her, but she told me, and I quote, 'next time you wake me up, I'm going to kill you.'"

There is an eery silence over the courtroom.

"I always tried to talk to her but she was a drunk." I sigh. "So around…December of my junior year, I came home from school and she had dropped a beer bottle in the kitchen. She told me to pick up the glass and I started cleaning it, and she checked my backpack. Now, back then I had a friend who was very selfish and she gave me one of her tests she had failed and she told me to get rid of it because she didn't want her Mom to see." I sigh. "Unluckily for me, my Mom saw. At this point, I threw out the glass, but my Mom freaked out. My Dad wasn't home, and I tried to tell her the test wasn't mine." I feel my baby starting to wake up in my belly and roll around and I put my hand on my stomach instinctively.

You're okay. I'm almost done.

"She attacked me. Slammed me into the wall in the kitchen and wrapped her hands around my throat."

I look up from the stand. "And she choked me until I passed out. I woke up when my Dad was home and she put me on the couch and covered me with a blanket. He thought I was napping." I feel my hands shaking. "I had never been more scared in my life, but I didn't tell my Dad what she had done because I didn't know what he was going to do. I knew he would never hurt a soul. But I was sixteen years old and I was terrified. I went up to my room, for a shower, and I started wondering why I was even alive, so I grabbed a bunch of medicine and mixed the pills. I put them in my mouth and right before I swallow them, my best friend texted me. To this day, he is the only reason I'm alive." I swallow the lump in my throat. "Two weeks later I was trying to get some water and my Mom was sleeping. Now, she told me not to wake her and then I was petrified she was going to murder me, so I was being as quiet as I could. I knew every single floorboard in that house that made sounds. I got my water and started heading back to my room when my cup slipped from my hand." I clear my throat again. "My Mom woke up, reminded me not to wake her up, and pinned me to the wall. She started choking me again, and I knew I was going to die this time." I put my hands on my belly to calm myself, and I can feel my little girl nudging around in there. "But my Dad walked into the living room and she ripped her off of me. He was very calm when he told me to go up to my room and pack a bag. He asked me to go to a friends house and not come back until the next day. I went to a friends house and called my best friend who was livid. When I got home the next day, my Dad told me he was filing for divorce and sole custody. He said I wasn't allowed to be home if he wasn't home, so I got a part time job and saved up money for a car." I pause. "After eight grueling months, he won the case. I was moving in with my Dad and my Mom went to rehab. Now, when you go through trauma like that...lets just say the affect of abuse are permanent. I woke up with nightmares every night, screaming. I didn't tell anybody, not even my best friend, because I was ashamed of feeling unsafe when I knew I was. After a while, my Dad decided we were moving to Daytona Beach, so I quit my job and we moved. I was reunited with my best friend after seven years, and I would wake up screaming, and my Dad never came in to check on me. I think he felt bad about everything that happened. I don't know, but my best friend was there. I was afraid to let people in. I was scared of dying alone...and then my best friend told me he was in love with me, which is a story for another time. Anyways, things were good for a while, but I had severe depression and anxiety, so after my best friend blamed my Dad for letting the abuse go on for as long as it did, my Dad put me in therapy, and I started to feel better, but I knew I wasn't. I bought a car with the money I saved and my Mom went to rehab. My Dad, for reasons I will never understand, stayed in contact with my Mom. He told me she was out of rehab and I figured she was healed, and I had a car and I thought I was a grownup because I was seventeen and seventeen year olds think they know everything." I clear my throat. "So I ran away, drove all the way up to Maryland in my old Jeep to visit my Mom. I blamed her for everything. I cried. She cried. I forgave her. My Dad came up to get me and I got better, you know? Things were awesome. I was in a healthy relationship and the nightmares were getting better, not gone, but better. I went off to college and I didn't stay in contact with my Mom solely because I didn't trust her. I forgave her, but forgetting it hard." I pause. "In my last year of college, Hurricane Adelaide ripped through. I'm sure you all remember how brutal it was." I pause. "At the time, I was at University of Miami with my at-the-time boyfriend slash best friend, so we drove back up to Daytona Beach and then met up with my Dad and my boyfriends parents. I was informed my Dad kept the house I was abused in Nd I had no other choice but to go back, so I did it and clung to my boyfriend. We got there and my Dad told me I wasn't allowed to be alone with my boyfriend, and, while I was only twenty one, a twenty one year old is old enough to be alone with a boy. I was in college." I pause. "I got into a fight with my Dad because I couldn't be alone with him, so I left with my boyfriend and went to Michigan." I sigh. "In Michigan, I got a call from my Dad telling me that he had a girlfriend, and I was happy for him at first, but then he said it was my Mom, and I got...well, I got mad, because after everything she did to me, he went back to her. It was like he never cared at all." I sigh. "And then he told me my Mom was five months pregnant and I was livid. I begged him to give the baby up for adoption because I told him that my mother was going to hurt my brother or sister." I sigh. "He wouldn't do it, so I told him I saw cutting him out of my life. I couldn't watch what happened to me happen to a sweet, innocent child." I sigh. "And after the hurricane I got back to Florida and my boyfriends parents were best friends with my Dad, and my boyfriends Mom told me she had overheard my Dad saying he was going to take me off the health insurance, take my car that I paid for, my cell phone, things like that, so I got my own plans for everything and went to his house to return my old phone, and again, asked him to give up the baby, but he refused and proceeded to tell me that all the abuse my mother had done to me was my fault because I didn't fight her off." I sigh. "After that, I had no contact for three years. I moved on, got engaged to my boyfriend, and then I was wondering about my parents and if I had a brother or sister, so my fiancé, his parents, and my cousin did a stakeout at their house." I pause. "And that was the first day I met Micah, because my parents went outside with Micah who was in a diaper and they went into the house and left him, at three years old, outside. A car was coming and I ran to grab him because he was going for the street, and then I picked him up and brought him to the door. My Dad answered and hid my from my Mom. He told my my Mom was crazy again, he said he couldn't leave yet because if he leaves when Micah is little, the court will favor the mother in terms of custody." I bite my lip. "He promised me he would reach out and that was the end of it. I had forgiven him for blaming me for the abuse." I wait. "I got married, built a house, and started my career alongside my husband, who has been by my side through all of this. I still get nightmares every now and again, and he's always there to hold me when I cry." I pause. "Anyways, a few weeks before Christmas, my doorbell rang. I was expecting somebody and when I pulled open the door, a child was standing on my porch in a t-shirt and shorts. It was thirty degrees outside. He said he was Micah and that I was his big sister. I brought him inside, shocked that he wasn't even dressed, and astounded at how thin he was. I could count every one of his ribs." I sigh sadly. "I used the number in his bag to call my father and he told me about the custody trial and asked me to look after Micah. My husband and I agreed. When on the phone with my father, I asked him how Micah got to my house in North Carolina, and he said he paid some guy to take a plane with him and then uber with him to my house. The man stayed in the car until I answered the door. I asked my Dad what would happen if they took him to the wrong house and he said, and I quote, 'Micah is smart.'"

I hear a few scoffs around the courtroom and shuffling of people that are pissed off by the situation at hand.

"I argued back and forth with my Dad and agreed to talk to my husband about it, who was right there when I was on the phone. Micah was in the living room with some relatives of ours." I sigh. "My husband and I agreed to watch him because if we didn't, he would be back with my Mom." I feel myself getting emotional again and my stomach juts out awkwardly as the baby moves around. "I asked what time Micah goes to bed and he told me he doesn't have a bedtime. I asked if he was in a booster seat and he said no. I asked what his grades are like and he said he didn't know. I asked if he ate dinner and he said he didn't know. I asked if he ate lunch and he said maybe, and that he didn't eat breakfast because he said he wasn't hungry, which my Dad later admitted he didn't know that, either."

Silence.

"And then he said he has nightmares. Later that night, I went through Micah's suitcase and found two pair of underwear, one was ripped and the other was fine. He has a shirt with stains and a shirt with holes, and two shorts. That was it. No toothbrush. Nothing. So I asked my brother when the last time he had a bath was because he smelled horrible, and he said he didn't know, that it was probably a few weeks ago. He proceeded to ask me if I was mad at him, and he started to cower away from me because he thought I was going to hit him." Clear my throat and blink away the tears. "I told him I wasn't our mother and I promised I wouldn't hurt him, and then I sent my husband to make him something to eat and I brought him upstairs for a bath. He has a small little hot wheels car, a yellow corvette with the paint chipping off, and he was running it along the walls of the tub. I let him play for a while and them I put soap on a washcloth and told him to wash up and he told me he didn't know how, that he didn't think he had ever been washed before." My voice cracks and I put my hand on my mouth to stop myself from crying. "So I sat there and instructed him on how to wash, and I washed his hair and put him in the only pair of underwear he had that weren't ruined and one of my shirts, and then I sent him downstairs to eat. My husband gave him grilled cheese and Micah asked for coffee."

"He asked for coffee?" The judge asks slowly.

"Yes. He said his Mom lets him drink it black. My husband gently told him little kids don't drink coffee and he said what he was supposed to drink, so my husband said water, milk, chocolate milk apple juice..." I trail off. "Micah asked for water, so after teaching him how to use manners, we got him water."

I look down and try my hardest to not start sobbing in front of everyone. I take a few deep breaths and sniffle a few times.

"And when my brother, at five years old, took a sip of that water, he was shocked, and he said 'wow, the kind my Mom gives me makes my throat burn.'"

I hear a few sniffles. My Dad remains neutral and my Mom is just looking down.

"I pulled my husband aside and we chose to lie down some rules to get him on some sort of schedule. We told him he will bathe every other day, he will go to sleep at eight every night, he will clean his own room, in which he told us he sleeps on the couch at my parents house." I sniffle. "We told him he will eat all three meals and that he had to promise to tell us when he got hungry. We told him we were going to the store to get him clothes and a seat for the car, and he got excited and asked me if he was allowed to have his own jacket." I sigh. "My Dad popped in after that, drove all the way to North Carolina to ask my husband and I for money." I take a deep breath. "And now I'm here, and your honor, I'm going to be frank with you." I stand up. "If you give custody of my little brother to my Mom, she's going to murder him. If you give custody of my little brother to my Dad, he's probably going to hurt Micah emotionally."

"Gracelyn, where is Micah right now?" the judge asks.

"Micah is in North Carolina with friends of my husband and I. He is safe. Since he has been with my husband and I, he gets good grades in school and he has gained twenty pounds, and he is finally in the same weight range that he should be for his height and age." I clear my throat. "He gets read bedtime stories every night and he knows how to wash himself in the bath tub. He doesn't have nightmares every night but when he does, he crawls into the bed with my husband and I. When Daniel and I first got him-"

"Who is Daniel?" The judge asks.

"My husband." I say. "When he and I first got Micah, I was up all night because I knew I was going to have nightmares. Micah woke from a nightmare and he told me he wished he was never born because nobody loves him. He told me he doesn't want to live with Mom and Dad ever again. He asked me to promise him that he wouldn't have to live with them, and I told him I was going to try my hardest to make sure that doesn't happen." I turn to the judge. "So now I'm here, seven months pregnant, trying to keep my word to my now six year old brother that he will never live with my Mom and Dad again." I pause. "And I have Micah's medical files to show you how his health was when we first got him in December and how his health is now. I have notes from my therapist back when I was sixteen. I have the amber alert file from when I ran away to visit my mother. I have the case files from my custody trial when I was in Micah's situation."

"I would like to see those." She says.

The officer takes the manila folder from me and hands it to the judge. I sit back down.

"I have my husband and his parents here, and they're willing to tell you what they witnessed through my struggled and Micah's.

She looks up from the papers.

"Your husband is here with you?" She asks.

"Yes ma'am." I say.

"I'd like for him to come up, too. You stay though. I want both of you."

I hear shuffling in the crowd and see Danny stand up, whispering to Beatrice as he hands her my purse, and then he walks up to the aisle and moves to stand next to me. I start to get up to give him my seat but he just shakes his head and stands next to me.

"What is your name?" The judge asks him.

"Daniel Grey." He says. I reach for his hand because I'm flipping out. He rubs his thumb across the back of it

What if what I told her wasn't enough? What if Micah ends up going with one of my parents?

"How long have you known the Levinsky household?"

"I've known them my entire life." He says. "My father and Scott were friends in college."

"So you were raised with your wife?"

"Yes ma'am."

"So you watched everything your wife just said happen? Either through the phone or in person?"

"Yes. I was there for almost everything that happened after she moved to Florida."

"Now I know what your wife thinks, but what do you think will happen if I give one of the Levinsky's custody of Micah?"

Danny blows out a breath.

"I think either way Micah will grow up very troubled. To be completely honest, I think if you give custody of Micah to Scott or Eileen, Micah will land himself in jail. He will use drugs. He will live a very, very troubled life. He will be beaten by his mother and dragged down by his father. While Scott wouldn't be the worst thing in the world, he is not cut out to be a parent. Neither one of them are."

"So what do you think should happen to Micah?"

"Your honor, my wife and I are willing to take him."

"You guys want custody?" She asks.

"Yes." We say in sync.

Everything is quiet and I squeeze Danny's hand anxiously.

"Your honor, if I may," Mom's lawyer stands up. "Why don't we ask the child what he wants?"

"The child has a name." The judge says. "And it is Micah. And Micah is in North Carolina." She turns to us. "I'm assuming Micah is at school right now?"

Danny looks at his watch and nods.

"Yes ma'am."

She looks at Mom's lawyer.

"So you want to pull the child out of school, find a way to get him down to Florida, and ask him himself?"

"It's Friday." Mom's lawyer says. "If they leave after school, they will be here by morning."

Are you fucking kidding me?

The judge looks hesitant for a while, and then she turns to Danny and I.

"Can it be arranged to bring Micah down here?"

Bullshit. This is bullshit.

"I'm sure we can work something out." Danny says, putting his hand on my shoulder and squeezing lightly.

Fuck this.

I stand up.

"So Mom, if you want him down here, are you going to chip in for air fare? Gasoline if they drive?"

She glares at me and I look at Dad. "And what about you?"

"I'm not chipping in because I know exactly what he's going to say." Dad says.

"And what's that?" The judge asks.

"I already asked Micah last time I drove up there if he wanted to come live with me, and he said he wanted to stay with my daughter and her husband."

Dad stands up and I hear his lawyer telling him to calm down.

"So there you go, Eileen! Look around you! Our little girl is pregnant with our grandchild and we'll probably never meet the baby! Danny and Grace got married, which, before your went haywire, that was your dream. We missed the wedding. Our six year old is terrified of you and he wants nothing to do with me because he knows that I'm associated with you. So congratulations Eileen, you have successfully ripped both of our kids away from us. You ripped apart Grace's life, you shredded Micah's childhood and you destroyed my adulthood. Are you happy, Eileen. Are you really happy?!"

My hands are shaking as I grip Danny's hand and hold on tightly.

Mom doesn't say anything, but her eyes linger on me and Danny, and then she sighs and mumbles something.

"What?" Dad asks loudly.

"I said no, Scott." She slams her hands down on the table she's sitting at and stands up. "I'm not happy, alright? I have a problem. Everyone knows it. Beer makes me angry. I relapsed. It happens!"

"That is not an excuse." Dad snaps.

"I'm not excusing it." She snaps. "Your honor, I don't want custody of Micah. He's safer with Scott or Grace. I'm a wreck, so send me to prison or rehab, I don't care, but don't give me Micah."

Dad's eyes land on me.

"Gracelyn, I know you're pissed at me and you probably always will-"

"No Scott, Gracelyn, your father asked you for money because I took all of his. Every penny of it. He's spent the last few months in a homeless shelter. He asked you for money because he literally had no other choice. Just forgive him, alright? He's a good guy and got trapped in all the messes I made. He's trying to right his wrongs."

My Dad has been in homeless shelters?

I rub my forehead.

"I wasn't going to say that." Dad says.

"Well she needed to know. Grace, you gotta stop punishing him for what I did, alright? He was just as shocked as you were. He's trying, okay? Just give him a chance."

"If you're dirt broke, how are you paying the lawyer?" Danny asks.

"I'm still working." Dad sighs. "Every penny I make goes toward the lawyer."

"Because if you can't go to court, Mom get's custody." I mutter.

"He sent Micah with a random guy because the guy was paying for his own ticket because he had to go up there anyways."

"The random guy had another kid with him." Dad adds.

"And the reason Micah didn't have a lot of stuff with him is because we couldn't afford it." Mom sighs. "Because I was spending all of our money on beer. The point is that, in this situation, your Dad didn't do anything but try to fix my messes."

Silence.

"Your honor, Micah does not need to come all the way down here." Dad says. "He wants to live with my daughter and her husband."

Nobody says anything and then slowly the judge nods.

"Alright. Gracelyn and Daniel have sole custody of Micah." She says. "However, I will give Scott visitation rights, but Gracelyn and Daniel choose when you get to see him. You can't show up at her house without an invitation."

That sounds fair to me.

"And you-" she points at Mom. "Have to go to rehab." She pauses. "Scott, if Eileen gets out of rehab and you go back to her, you will lose all visitation rights of Micah."

She hits her hammer thing down on the stand. "This trial is over."

The moment those words leave her mouth, I'm on my feet and walking out of the courtroom.

I can't handle this shit for another minute. I'm going to be sick.

I can feel the baby moving around in my belly as I turn into the restroom.

I rush into a stall and shut the door, and then I start throwing up.

I usually throw up because of stress with my pregnancy.

After a few moments of this, I straighten up and flush the toilet, and then I rinse my mouth out.

I keep a toothbrush and toothpaste in my purse, but Beatrice has it.

I hear people entering the bathroom, and then everyone gets kind of quiet, causing me to stiffen.

"Beatrice." Mom says to her former best friend.

"Eileen." Beatrice replies.

I want to get out of this courthouse right the fuck now.

I push open the stall door and see Beatrice facing me with my purse in hand.

Neither one of them are talking but some of the ladies that were in the crowd of the trial are watching the exchange.

I walk over to Beatrice and she holds my purse so I can dig through it. I grab my toothbrush and toothpaste and wet my toothbrush, watching both of them in the mirror as I start to brush my teeth.

"I assume you're taking care of my daughter?" Mom asks finally.

"I have been since you quit." Beatrice says coldly.

Mom nods slowly.

"Alright."

With that, she walks out.

I spit the foam in my mouth into the sink and rinse my toothbrush.

I put the toothbrush and toothpaste back into the little plastic baggie it was in, and I zip it up, and then I hand it to Beatrice who drops it into my purse.

"Are you okay?" She asks.

"I want to get the hell out of here." I mutter.

"So let's go."

*****

It took a few minutes to get to my Jeep after we signed custody papers for , and now we're all driving through Daytona Beach. We checked out of the hotel before we left for the courthouse. The car seat for the baby is in the back just in case, but the trunk, so Beatrice and Caleb have space.

My eyes stay on the window, my hands resting on my belly. The baby isn't moving right now, so she's probably sleeping.

"Grace?" Danny asks suddenly.

"Hmm?" I hum.

"I don't like the name Mariposa anymore."

I turn my head from the window to my husband.

"Why not?"

"I don't know. I just don't see us yelling for Mariposa to come do dishes. It's a cute name, but I don't like it."

"How long have you felt this way?" I ask.

"A while..." he trails off.

I look down at my belly.

"Well now we have to pick another name."

"I know." He says. "I'm sorry."

"It's fine." I look down at my belly for a moment, and then I sigh and look back to the window.

I see a man walking down the street with a dirty suitcase in nice pants and a button down shirt, and then I realize that man is my father.

"Oh god." I whisper.

"What?" Danny asks.

Beatrice and Caleb are watching him in silence, and Danny glances over.

"Shit." He mutters.

While I'm still very confused and haven't had time to think about it, I know we have to help him.

"Danny." I mumble.

"I'll pull over." He says.

We gets over into the right lane and turns into a Dollar General parking lot.

Dad is right in front of the store and he obviously has no idea it's us.

We all kind of sit there not knowing what to do, and then I unbuckle my seatbelt and get out.

"Dad!" I call.

His head whips to the side at the sound of my voice, and then he starts walking towards me.

He stops a few feet away from me.

"Where's your truck?" I ask

He rubs the back of his neck.

"Uh, your Mom took it."

"She had a car." I say.

"Yeah but she totaled it." He clears his throat.

I feel my stomach growl and the baby wakes up and starts to wiggle around.

I woke her up.

"Where are you going?" I ask him.

"Uh...back to the shelter. I'm going to try to save up money for an apartment...but my credit isn't great so we'll see."

"How do you eat?"

"Well they have food there..." he trails off.

It physically hurts to see him like this.

"Do you want to go get food?" I ask him.

"Oh no, that's fine-"

"We'll pay." Danny says, leaning over from the drivers seat so he can see him.

"No really, I'm okay." Dad says.

Caleb rolls the window down in the backseat.

"Stop being stubborn and get in the car." He says.

Dad looks hesitant but he gives in. I walk to the back and open up the trunk, revealing the grey and pink car seat.

I see his eyes linger on it but he doesn't say anything, he just puts his suitcase in and walks around to the back seat. Caleb scoots into the middle and Dad gets into the seat behind mine.

I get into the front seat and put my seatbelt on, and we're all quiet as Danny drives.

Finally, he breaks the silence.

"Where should we go?"

All I can think about is steak and shake.

"We should go to steak and shake." I say.

"We go there all the time." Danny says.

"Yeah because I want milkshakes all the time."

He glances at me and sighs.

"Alright, fine. Steak and shake it is."

*****

I actually need more Danlyn scenes so yeah those are probably coming~Sam

Chapter Twelve: Wrestling

Chapter Twelve: Wrestling

We're all sitting at the table and nobody really knows what to say, but everyone is watching me pour the french fry seasoning all over my fries. I suck on my milkshake and the moment I swallow, I feel the thick cold liquid slide down my throat, and the baby begins to kick. I look down at my belly and sigh because it hurts slightly, and she's holding her foot against the top of my stomach. I reach down and tap her little foot and it disappears and moment later, and then she starts kicking the shit out of me.

"Are you okay?" Beatrice laughs.

"I'm being internally abused." I say, but I'm not mad. I love it when she kicks, even if it hurts me sometimes, because that means she healthy.

"She seems to be moving a lot more than she was last week." Danny says.

"That's because she's running out of space." I say, cringing as she kicks again.

"Have you picked out names?" Dad asks quietly.

"Well we did." I look at my husband. "But he decided that he doesn't like her name anymore."

Danny shrugs.

"I have no shame."

My little girl kicks again and I smile.

I love my little angel.

"You know, if you were a girl, we were going to name you Emily." Beatrice says.

"Emily." I look down at my belly and she kicks again. "I actually love that name."

"Yeah, that's cute. I can see that."

"Emily Juliet Grey. That's beautiful."

Our parents start nodding.

"How should we spell it?" Danny asks.

Sighing, I grab a napkin and get a pen from my purse.

"Either traditionally like E-M-I-L-Y." I write it down. "Or like E-M-I-L-E-E."

I show it to Danny.

"I like the first one." Danny says.

I nod, studying the different variations.

"Me too." I decide. "People are always going to spell it that way anyways."

"We can call her Emmy." Danny says.

I nod in agreement and we all fall back into the awkward silence.

I start snack on my french fries, zipping them in my milkshake, sucking down the milkshake.

I'm just so hungry.

When I finish mine, I start to eye Danny's.

He's hardly touched it.

"Are you gonna have that?" I ask, pointing to his milkshake.

He looks at me and sighs.

"We can share it." He says, sliding it between the two of us.

I start sucking his down too, snagging a few fries off of his plate and using them to dip into his milkshake.

He looks amused, and I know I really should be thinking about my Dad right now.

I can't just let him go back to a homeless shelter.

Danny and I could get him a small apartment until he can afford it hims elf...but does he want to stay down here or move somewhere else?

I thought he needed money for his own selfish reasons. I didn't realize he needed it because he was going to be homeless.

If he moves to North Carolina, we can get him a small two bedroom apartment and maybe he can see Micah.

I definitely could let him stay with Danny and I, but we have a six year old and Beatrice and Caleb, and a newborn on the way.

I feel like I need to apologize for treating him so horribly. I didn't realize how much he was struggling.

And it's all Mom's fault. Everything is always Mom's fault.

I told him I forgave him, but I don't think I really did.

I always resented him for getting with Mom, but what happened to me and Micah wasn't any more his fault than it was ours. Mom is crazy, and she's the one I should be mad at.

I swallow a fry and take a sip of my water.

"Dad, can I talk to you outside?" I ask.

He looks a little surprised but he nods.

I stand up and he does too, walking with me out of the restaurant.

I move away from the door and sigh, nudging a rock with my foot.

"I don't really know how to say this so I'm just going to come right out with it." I say. He nods and waits. "For the past few years...I have blamed you for everything. I was struggling with what happened to me and I was pissed you got back with Mom, but you were there for me. If I told you I needed help, you would have helped me. I know that now. I know you stayed away when I was having nightmares because you felt bad, and I understand. When Danny explained to you how bad off I really was, you did help. You were there back when Danny and I were fighting before we started dating. You stayed on top of me and made sure I had good grades. You helped me pay for college, and I don't know why you said some of the things you did, I don't know why you were going to take me off of the health insurance and stuff...but something tells me if was all Mom, wasn't it?"

"I don't know." He says. "Taking you off the plans was her, but I don't know why I told you it was your fault. It definitely wasn't your fault."

"Well either way, I know you didn't mean it, and I've just...missed you so much." I take a deep breath. "And I think it's taken me seeing you at your lowest possible level still fighting for Micah to snap out of it and realize that everything that has happened isn't any more your fault than it is mine is Micah's. I'm sorry for how cold I have been towards you, and I understand you're trying."

"No kiddo, it really is my fault." He says. "I knew she wasn't okay. I didn't do anything about it."

"But you did." I whisper. "You did. You got me away from her. You got Micah away from her. In the end, you did the right thing, and something tells me that you knew you weren't getting custody back after you gave him to me and Danny."

He looks down.

"Micah deserves better than a shit father that's living in a shelter." He laughs a little.

"You're not a shit father." I whisper. "You've struggled just as bad as Micah and I have."

He nods slowly.

"I'm sorry, Dad." I whisper.

"It's not your fault kid." He says. "But it's okay."

I lean forward and wrap my arms around his waist. He hugs me back.

After a few seconds, we pull away.

"I'm sorry for everything Grace." He whispers.

"I know." I pat his shoulder. "Let's go back inside."

Danny looks super curious as to what we were talking about and I know he's going to question me.

Before Dad sits down, I gesture for my husband to follow me, and this time I go outside with him.

"What were you guys talking about?" He asks.

"I just...Danny, this isn't his fault. It's my Mom. Everything comes down to my Mom being an alcoholic.

He sighs.

"I know Grace, I know that, but it's just that you just found out the truth, and I don't want him moving in with us."

"I don't think he should move in with us." I whisper. "I think we should get him an apartment."

"You want to pay for an apartment for him?"

"Just until he can pay for it himself." I nod.

"We have to find an apartment first." He says.

"He can stay with us until then. I can't just leave him on the street."

"Grace, you know how I feel about your Dad. He got himself into this mess by going back to your Mom."

"I know." I say, putting my hands on his chest. "I know baby, but if he didn't, we wouldn't have Micah."

"I know sweetheart, and you know I love Micah, but this is your Dad's fault."

"It's my Mom's fault too. It's mostly my Mom's fault."

"Grace, I don't trust him." He says.

"You don't have to trust him." I say.

"Actually, I do. I don't trust him around Micah, I don't trust him around Emily, and I sure as hell don't trust him around you."

"Just give him a chance. Everyone deserves a second chance."

"He had a second change." Danny says.

"Please do this for me." I whisper. "We can afford it."

He stays quiet, studying me for a long time.

"Fine." He says. "But if he does one thing out of line, he's out Grace, I'm not kidding."

"Okay." I say. "Thank you."

"This is if he agrees to move to North Carolina. If he doesn't-"

"We get him an apartment down here."

He sighs.

"If he moves up with us, I'm not buying him a new car. He can get his own transportation."

"Okay."

"And he better find a job."

*****

It took a lot of begging to get him to agree, and he eventually gave in with the promise to pay us back every penny.

We dropped my Dad and Danny's parents off at him and then put Micah's booster seat back in the car to bring him home. It's eight thirty and he's fast asleep in bed, but it wasn't us to gave him his bedtime story tonight, it was my Dad.

We sat on the couch with him and Beatrice and Caleb and watched a movie and now we're in bed. It's past midnight and we just made love for the first time in a week. I think one of our parents are still awake. Beatrice and Caleb were in the room across the hall from Micah, but today we politely asked them if they could move downstairs because tomorrow, we're removing all the furniture in the room across from Micah to start the nursery.

They took their things and went down to the room under the one they're already in. Dad is across the hall from them until we get him an apartment.

Now my bare backside is pressed against the front of Danny, and he's tracing patterns on my arm. I feel him place a few kisses on my shoulder.

"Can I ask you something?" I whisper.

"Of course." He murmurs.

"What's going to happen to us if...after Emily is born, I get saggy breasts and I have a lose belly?"

His fingertips on my arm pause slightly, and I hear him shift.

"What do you mean?"

"What if I never get my body back? I'm having a baby Danny, and bodies after babies aren't really that attractive."

"Oh princess." He kisses my shoulder. "I was never with you for your body. Big or small, tall or short, I will love you either way. I'm not with you because you're beautiful, I'm with you because I love you. I love your personality and who you are as a person. That's why I fell in love with you."

"You told me you fell in love with me for my eyes."

"That was a factor." He laughs softly. "When I was little, my Mom told me to fall in love with a girl for her eyes, because that's the only thing that never changes."

I carefully roll over to face him, pulling the blanket up higher to cover my breasts.

"Your Mom thinks I'm going to be one of those Mom's that loses all the baby weight within two months." I admit.

"Well either way baby, I'm going to love you just as much, maybe even more than I do now."

I lean forward to kiss him and my arm brushes against my breast. I feel something wet, so I reach over and turn on the light, sitting up.

There is a strand of white liquid coming out of my breast, and it looks like semen.

"Did you shoot onto my boobs?" I whisper to Danny. He props himself up with his elbow and shakes his head.

"No. What is that stuff?"

"Oh my god, do you think it's milk?" I ask.

"I don't know. Why would you be leaking? You're still pregnant."

"What if something is wrong?" I ask. "What if I'm going into labor?!"

We both kind of sit there and Emily isn't moving.

In a hurry, I get out of bed and pull on pajama pants and one of Danny's shirts. He gets on sweatpants and follows me downstairs. Caleb is still awake, flipping through the TV.

"Is Mom up?" Danny asks.

"She went to bed." He says. "Why?"

His eyes linger on my messy hair and he wrinkles his nose slightly, probably knowing exactly what we were doing upstairs.

Danny follows me to the bedroom and he pushes the door open. I can see Beatrice sleeping but he walks right up to her and starts shaking her.

"Mom! Mom!"

"What Daniel?!" She grumbles. "Leave me be! I'm sleeping."

He gets the same way when he's woken too. It's good to know he gets it from somewhere.

"Mom, I think Grace is going into labor but I don't know." Danny says.

That makes her sit up.

"What?" She asks, throwing the covers off of her. "No, she's only twenty nine weeks. She has to make it eight more weeks."

"I know but I don't know." Danny says. "Should I take her to the hospital?"

"Where is she?"

"She's right there." Danny points towards me. She stands up, rubbing her face.

"Let's go into the living room." She says, grabbing her glasses.

She walks past me and Danny keeps his hands on my shoulders as we walk.

I look down at my shirt and there are two round wet spots where my nipples are leaking.

"Look!" Danny points to my shirt. "She's leaking milk! Isn't that a sign of preterm labor? She can't have Emily yet! It's too soon!"

Beatrice's eyes linger on my hair.

"Did you guys just have sex?" She asks.

"Yes..." Danny trails off.

Beatrice sighs. "You're twenty nine weeks. Having sex can...stimulate things." She itches her head uncomfortably. "If you were sucking on things..." she trails off.

Oh god. Danny sucking on my nipples made me lactate.

"Did I just breastfeed from my wife?" Danny whispers.

"No, but you made her lactate."

Silence.

"You probably shouldn't suck on them because it can trigger hormones that will jumpstart labor." Caleb says without removing his eyes from the TV.

I look at him.

"That's why you were two weeks early." Caleb says, glancing at his son.

Danny cringes and then nods.

"Alright."

"Oh, and Grace?" Caleb asks.

"Yeah?"

"Your shirt is see through."

I put my hands on my breasts.

"Dad!" Danny says.

"What?! I wasn't looking for it, but it's hard to notice when she's wearing a white shirt! It stands out!"

I sigh and walk into the kitchen. I get a bottle of cold water.

"I'm going to bed." I announce.

"No, are you having any pain?" Beatrice asks.

"I'm having pain from your husband looking at my tits." I joke.

"I wasn't looking!" Caleb laughs.

"Uh, you did mention that her nipples were showing." Danny says.

"Because they were!" He says, outraged. He puts the footrest down on the couch and stands up. The remote is in his lap and it clatters loudly to the floor. I feel Emily jump in my belly and start to squirm.

"You scared the baby!" I exclaim.

"The baby is inside of you!" Caleb starts laughing.

"God Dad, when the baby comes and you wake her up, you're going to take care of her." Danny says.

"I can't! I don't have nipples."

"Oh really? You don't have nipples?" Beatrice snickers.

"Shut up, you know that's not what I meant." Caleb scowls. "The only one who can take care of her is you. I did my time with this one." He swats at my husband, who pretends to swing at Caleb.

"Oh, you wanna go?" Caleb says. "I brought you into this world, I can take you out."

"You won't do it." Danny says.

Caleb lunges at Danny, knocking him to the ground.

They start to wrestle.

"Boys!" Beatrice says. "That's enough, both of you! Somebody is going to end up hurt!"

I hear a bedroom door shut and my Dad comes walking into the living room in a pair of sweatpants, rubbing his eyes.

He looks at the two grown men on the floor and I watch as Caleb pins Danny down and tries to give him a wet Willy, but Danny shoves him off of him and springs to his feet, ready to fight.

Caleb grabs Danny's biceps and Danny grabs Caleb's and they both try to take each other down and end up flipping over the couch.

"I'm going to bed." I say, rolling my eyes. "Caleb, please don't kill my-"

They flip over so Danny is on top and Caleb rolls to the side, knocking Danny off the couch. His head slams against the metal coffee table and I hear a loud bang.

"Oh shit." Caleb sits up. "Are you alright?"

"Yeah, I'm fine." Danny mumbles, but he takes his hand to the back of his head, and when he pulls it away, it's dark red. "Oh." He says. "Maybe I'm not."

*****

I'm so mean

~Sam

Chapter Thirteen: Sexist

Chapter Thirteen: Sexist

They flip over so Danny is on top and Caleb rolls to the side, knocking Danny off the couch. His head slams against the metal coffee table and I hear a loud bang.

"Oh shit." Caleb sits up. "Are you alright?"

"Yeah, I'm fine." Danny mumbles, but he takes his hand to the back of his head, and when he pulls it away, it's dark red. "Oh." He says. "Maybe I'm not."

"You're bleeding." Caleb says.

"Yeah, actually Dad, judging by the amount of blood on my hand, I kind of figured that I was bleeding."

"Smartass." Caleb grumbles, pushing himself up from the couch. "You probably need some stitches. Damn, I thought you were a man Daniel. You got your ass kicked by a forty five year old."

"Shut up Dad." Danny snaps. "I may be bleeding, but I can still fight you."

"Oh really?" Caleb laughs.

"Yeah." Danny pushes himself up onto his feet and turns around to face his Dad.

I maneuver around the couch and push my way between them.

"No." I say. "You're done. We're going to tie something around your head and then we're going to the hospital."

"We don't need to go to the hospital. We can use a stapler." Dad says.

"Yeah, Scott's right. Why pay a hefty hospital bill?" Caleb agrees.

"There's a stapler in the junk drawer in the kitchen." Danny nods.

"I'll go get it." Dad says.

I look at Beatrice with a shocked look.

"I'll be fine. Just hold me down and do it quick. Once my skin starts growing over the staples, we rip them out." Danny says.

"Agreed." Caleb nods.

Dad returns with the stapler and I snatch it out of his hand.

"You want to do it?" Danny asks.

"No, I don't want to do it!" I exclaim. "You guys are idiots! All three of you!"

"Come on, give me the stapler." Danny says, holding his hand out.

"No." I hand it to Beatrice.

"Ma, come on." Danny whines. "Just give me the stapler."

I go get a towel from the laundry room and go back to the living room, tying it around Danny's head.

He pouts the entire time.

"Grace, I'm not going."

"If I cracked my head open, would you let me use a stapler at home?" I ask.

He hesitates.

"Well no, but that's different. You're a girl and you guys can't handle pain."

"Oh?" I laugh. "We can't?"

"No, you can't." Caleb scoffs.

Beatrice's eyebrows shoot up, but Dad just presses his lips together and mutters, "You guys better stop. It's a trap."

"I'm about to push your fucking baby out of my vagina." I snap at my husband. "Something this big." I connect my fingertips of both hands to make a circle. "Is coming out of something this big." I make a circle with my index finger and thumb, and then I throw the staplers on the couch. "Next time you act sexist, I will make you sleep on the couch or on the bed in the basement for a week. I'm not kidding. Now you're not being an idiot and stapling your head at home! We're going to the hospital!"

Pissed off, I grab one of his jackets off the railing on the stairs and pull it on. I shove my feet in my flip flops and grab the keys to the car. "Now let's go!" I point towards the basement stairs with my other hand on my hip.

He doesn't even try to argue, he just walks past me onto the stairs.

*****

To be completely honest, I'm mad at Danny.

I'm mad that he got hurt, because now I lost a ton of sleep. I'm mad that he's sexist, and I'm mad that he didn't apologize for calling me, Beatrice, and every other woman on the planet weak.

I won't be childish and ignore him, but I'm not going to pretend not to be mad either.

I'm trying my hardest to be nice but I'm so mad that he was so sexist and rude.

I feel Emily squirming in my belly as I walk across the hall to Emily's room.

They're painting it right now but as I peek inside, the vision I originally had for the nursery has changed, and I know that the light grey color won't work.

This wouldn't be the first time I've changed my mind. Sometimes it looks better in my head. I've had him and the team repaint the entire exterior of a house before.

"Uh oh." I say, leaning against the doorframe.

Danny freezes, turning around with a roller in his hand.

"Don't say it." He pleads.

"It's too dark."

"What's too dark?" Dad asks.

"The paint."

"Well it's already on the wall." Caleb says.

"It needs to be white." I say.

Dad and Caleb look outraged.

"No." Caleb says. "t's on the wall already."

"I'm telling you right now, it's not going to work." I argue, stepping back slightly. I'm not supposed to be breathing paint fumes like that because the chemicals are bad for the baby. "Change it to white."

Danny drops his roller into the tray.

"What shade?"

"We're seriously changing the color?" Caleb asks.

"I don't know how to explain it, but she knows what she's doing. If she says it needs to be white, it needs to be white."

He turns to me.

"Let's go to the basement and pick the right shade."

He walks out and I follow him, wadding down the stairs.

The entire time, I glare at him because I'm so mad.

Maybe it's because I'm pregnant and just angry all the time, but I'm so mad.

We stop in the garage where all the paint is.

We have a lot of paint, and there are a lot of different shades.

"I want this one for the wall." I point to one that is the same color as milk. "And this one." I tap one that's a whitish-grey. "I want this one for the window."

"Okay." He says.

"Okay thanks."

I turn around and walk out without a word.

I go back upstairs. Beatrice, I've noticed, seems to be avoiding the guys and I decide to rant to her and see if she's just as pissed as I am.

I walk over to where she's sitting at the breakfast table. She has a mug of coffee next to her and her iPad is resting on the table.

She's looking at a co sleeper crib that goes next to a bed.

She glances up when she hears me approach.

"Have you and Danny thought about having Emily in your bedroom for the first couple of months?" She wonders.

"We want her in the crib." I say.

"I really think you would benefit from having her in the bedroom. I don't know anybody that didn't have the baby in the room with them. It's much easier and you get more sleep."

I cringe.

"I don't know if I want to do that."

"You don't have to, but you might benefit from having a sleeper just in case. It would suck to struggle with Emmy until you can get to the store."

She's probably right.

"Okay, but I don't want one of those that puts the baby in the bed with us. I'm afraid I'll roll on top of her or a blanket will cover her face."

"I put Danny in a bassinet right next to my bed." She says. "It's much safer."

I nod slowly.

"Maybe later we can go to the store with Danny?" She suggests.

"Or we can go now and ditch our sexist husbands." I mutter.

She takes a sip of her coffee, her eyes staying on me, and then she sets the cup down.

"You're mad too?"

I take the opportunity to have somebody to be mad with me and sit down.

"I'm pissed." I whisper. "I'm about to push a baby out of my hoohah and he was flipping out for a needle to numb him!"

She scowls and rolls her eyes.

"Let's take his truck and go shopping. And let's go to lunch. They can stay home."

"Great idea. I'll tell them we can get Micah too."

"Okay. Let me go get dressed."

"Yeah, me too."

*****

This chapter was so boring I'll try to make the next chapter more interesting

~Sam

Chapter Fourteen: Family Lawyer

Chapter Fourteen: Family Lawyer

"Honestly, the worst part is probably that he didn't even apologize." I say, putting another Babies R Us bag in the car. "If he had apologized, I would get over it, but he hasn't."

"He wasn't raised that way." She shakes her head.

"Well he won't apologize. He's stubborn. He's been that way since birth." I exclaim.

"Oh, I know. I raised him." She says. "You're just as stubborn as he is."

"Yeah, but at least I know when to apologize." I exclaim.

"Oh sweetheart, Danny knows when to apologize. I think he genuinely thinks he did nothing wrong."

I frown.

I know he's a good guy and I know he apologizes when he knows he did something wrong, so the fact that he hasn't yet tells me he really doesn't know he did something.

Wow.

Beatrice gets in the drivers seat of Danny's truck and I get into the passenger seat, buckling up.

Now the fact that he doesn't know he did something wrong makes me even more pissed off.

My phone chimes with a message.

Hubby: HiMe: Hi?Hubby: where did you and mom go

We have been gone for three hours.

Me: we left three hours ago

Hubby: oh okay where did you go

Me: shopping.

I see him read the message and he starts typing, and then he stops, and then he starts again, and then he stops. Nearly two minutes pass before the typing symbol comes up again.

Hubby: are you mad at me or something? You're acting weird

Me: no.

I really should just put a stop to this.

Me: actually yes. I'm pissed

It goes to read right away.

Hubby: oh

Hubby: can we talk when you get home please?

I know communication is key to a healthy relationship and I don't like how it feels to be mad at him.

Me: yes

Hubby: I love you princess

I rub my forehead and sigh.

Me: I love you too

I turn my attention to the window and watch as Beatrice drives to Micah's school.

My phone vibrates and I look down at the message.

Hubby: I'm freaking out lol

Hubby: like how mad are you? Because idk what I did

Me: I'm mad

Hubby: yes but why

Me: we can talk about it when I get home I'm pulling into Micah's school

Hubby: speaking of Micah we need to talk about him

Me: ok when I get home

Hubby: okay

We reach the spot where all the kids are and Micah runs up to the trunk and the safety patrol opens the back door.

He clambers into the truck, tossing his backpack somewhere in the backseat.

"Hi." He says.

"Hey bud, how was school?" I ask, turning to make sure he puts his seatbelt on. He clicks it into place.

"It was cool. I got to go outside and we planted a seed for a science project."

"That's good." I say. "Do you have homework?"

"Yeah." He says.

He turns his attention to the window.

"Grace, Dad came to stay. Does that mean Mom is coming too?"

"No." I say right away. "Mom isn't coming over ever."

"But she can, right? Because she has custody of me?"

I hesitate.

"Micah, how do you know what custody is?"

"I heard you and Danny talking about it." He shrugs.

I sigh.

"Micah, it's not right to listen to conversations."

"Well it was about me." He says.

I shake my head.

"Micah, Mom and Dad don't have custody of you anymore. Me and Danny do. That means we're in charge of you. If we don't want Mom around you, Mom isn't allowed around you."

He doesn't answer me for a long time, and then right when we turn into our neighborhood, he speaks up.

"Do you think it's possible for somebody to have parents that aren't their real parents by blood?" He wonders.

I hesitate.

"Yes."

Beatrice and I exchange glances.

"Oh. Okay." He smiles a little.

"Why?" I ask.

"Well just Kyle and Miley are my parents, that's all."

Beatrice stops the car in the garage and Micah unbuckles his seatbelt and grabs his backpack, getting out in a hurry.

"It's snack time!" He exclaims, running into the house.

Beatrice and I sit there in shock.

I force myself to unbuckle my seatbelt and walk in the house.

I shut the garage door with the button and go upstairs with Beatrice.

"Do you think you can give him a snack?" I ask my mother-in-law. "I need to go talk to Danny."

"Yeah." She says quietly.

She knew Miley and Kyle wanted custody and I did too, but Danny and I were planning on keeping Micah.

I mean, he's ours now. We have custody.

With a heavy heart, I drag myself up to the second story, which is kind of the third.

Emily's room is painted the colors I asked them to change it to, and they all look up when I peek into the room.

Danny stands up quickly when he realizes I'm home.

"Do you like it?" He asks.

They left the crown mounding white, which is now the same color as the edges of the windows, which looks good.

"Looks good." I say. "I need to talk to you."

"Yeah, I know." He mumbles.

He already looks like a scolded child and I feel slightly bad, but if he wasn't sexist, this wouldn't be a conversation I have to have with him.

But now I'm more worried about Micah than anything.

I turn around and cross the hallway balcony to our bedroom. I hear him following me and when he walks in, I shut the door.

He looks nervous.

I step around him and walk further into the bedroom, sitting down on the bed. I run my fingers through my hair and sigh.

He shoves his hands in his pockets and waits for it.

"You're sexist." I say, and his eyebrows raise.

"What?"

"You are sexist." I repeat. "And what you said last night about how girls can't handle pain? That's rude and insulting and your Mom is pissed about it too. You are sexist, Danny. I'm about to push our baby out of my body. And I just-do you actually think girls can't handle pain?"

"Of course not, Grace. Last night I was being an idiot and messing around. You women take a lot more pain than guys do. And when you're sick you still get up and do stuff, which I'll never understand. I'm sorry baby, I was being as asshole and I didn't mean it."

I sigh slowly and nod.

"Okay."

"That's it?" He asks.

"Yes, but I've been mad about it all day."

"Why didn't you talk to me sooner?" He wonders.

"I don't know. I'm petty." I throw my hands up. "We have more pressing issues than this."

"Which is?"

"Micah, Danny." I whisper. "Micah."

He studies me for a long time.

"Something tells me you know exactly what I'm going to tell you." He whispers.

I look down.

"What were you going to tell me?" I whisper.

He sits down next to me on the bed and puts his arm around my shoulder. I rest my head on his shoulder and sigh.

"Last night when I was giving Micah a bath, or rather, watching him while he got a bath, I was showing him how to pull the plug on the drain and how you flip the switch and he said, and I quote, 'at my dad's house, you push on the drain and it sucks out all the water' but obviously I got confused because he didn't get baths at your Dad's house, and I was going to ask him who he was talking about and then he said, 'well I don't know if he's actually my Dad but I think he is' and baby, he was talking about Kyle."

I nod my head against his shoulder.

"In the car he asked me if it's possible to have parents that aren't your blood and I told him yes because kids get adopted all the time, and he was smiling and stuff so I asked him why he asked me that and he told me that that Kyle and Miley are his parents. And apparently he listens to our conversations? Because he knows about custody and he knew that my parents had custody, so I told him that you and I have custody now."

Danny sighs softly and starts rubbing my back.

"So what do you want to do?" He murmurs.

"I want to be selfish and keep him." I mumble. "But Micah doesn't want that. Every child deserves loving parents. If I could pick between loving parents and my sister and her husband, I would pick the parents."

He nods slowly.

"What about your Dad? He has visitation rights."

"Maybe if we invite Kyle and Miley over and see how they interact with Micah, Dad will see it."

"Yeah." He mutters.

"Danny, what if we give them custody and they move away?"

"I don't think they will. We can set down ground rules."

"Yes, but if we pass off custody to them and they legally adopt him, our rules don't matter. He'll be their child."

"Your father has visitation rights." Danny reminds me. "They can't go very far."

That's true.

"Okay, I just want to see how they act. What is so different between what they're doing and what we're doing?"

"Alright, I'll call them up."

*****

We asked Beatrice not to say anything and she just said she wouldn't have said anything anyways.

I explained to Miley and Kyle the situation with my Dad and they said they're going to be good about it.

When the doorbell rings, my heart leaps into my throat.

Micah doesn't know they're coming over, but he's sitting at the kitchen table with me and he's zipping through his homework quickly.

Danny goes to get the door. Caleb and Beatrice are making dinner and my Dad is on his old laptop. I think he's applying for a ton fo jobs.

I hear Danny greeting them and the second I hear Miley's voice, Micah's head snaps up. I hear Kyle and Miley laugh at something Danny said and Micah gets the biggest smile I've ever seen on his face and he gets out of his seat and goes running across the house in his socks.

Pepper jumps up to follow him.

"Hiiiiiiiii!" Micah throws his arms around both of their legs, and I hear them laughing. "Come sit with me! I'm doing homework!"

He grabs their hands and drags both of them across the house to the kitchen.

Dad is watching the situation play out, his eyes slightly narrowed, but he doesn't say anything about it. He stands up to shake their hands and I start to get up to greet them but Miley waves me off.

"Don't get up." She bends down to hug me.

When she pulls away, Kyle puts his hand on my shoulder.

"How's motherhood treating you?" He smiles.

"I'm ready to have the baby." I laugh.

"I think we're all ready to meet her." Miley smiles.

Micah is watching everyone start talking about the weather and the usual formal greetings and I see his eyes going back and forth between everyone in the room and then he walks over to his homework, answers the last two questions and puts the sheet in his homework folder. He puts the folder in his backpack and walks out, and when he comes back, he has a box of his legos that "Santa" got him for Christmas.

He stops right in front of Kyle and completely interrupts mid conversation.

"Will you play with me?"

"Sure little man." Kyle sets his phone and keys on the table and Micah sets the box on the floor.

They sit down out of the way and Kyle gives Micah his undivided attention. I notice Miley occasionally glancing over at them as they start building something.

Everyone seems to be noticing the way Micah is acting, and then they start talking about Emily and then Dad asks Miley if her and Kyle plan of having any children.

I mentally facepalm and watch the happiness completely vanish from Miley's face. Kyle's attention diverts from Micah to his wife, and he stands up.

"Oh uh," Miley clears her throat. "I actually can't have any kids..." she trails off.

"Oh, I'm so sorry." Dad says. "I never should have asked."

"No, it's okay." Miley says. "People ask me that a lot actually..." she trails off.

I never actually knew why aside from that she was infertile.

"Why not, if you don't mind me asking?" Dad asks.

"I had a cyst on one of my ovaries and the doctor said I couldn't have any kids...so."

"I'm sorry." Dad says.

"It's alright." She smiles sadly.

"Dad!" Micah exclaims impatiently.

"Yes?" My Dad looks at him, and Micah's face screws up in confusion.

"I'm not talking to you. I'm talking to my Dad Kyle."

Kyle's eyes widen slightly and he looks at my Dad. The house is dead silent and I swear even Emily can feel how quickly the tensions rise in the room.

"I'm sorry." Kyle says. "I didn't-I don't-Micah, I'm not your Dad buddy, he's your Dad." He gestures to my father, and Kyle is rubbing his neck anxiously.

"Uh, Grace said it's possible to have parents that aren't blood related." Micah says smartly. "So that makes you and Miley my parents."

Everyone looks at me and I laugh nervously.

"Kids get adopted all the time." I mutter. I reach across the table and grab Danny's water.

"You guys are my parents, right?" Micah whispers, and he looks scared for the answer.

In his mind, he has a good Mom and a good Dad.

"Gracelyn, can I speak to you please?" Dad says. "Alone."

Shitfuckshitfuckshitfuck

"Yeah." I push myself up from the table and follow him outside. He walks with me down the steps and leads the way down to the boardwalk, all the way to the end.

"This is a long walk for somebody who is seven months pregnant." I grumble, putting my hand on my big belly as I reach the cover on the balcony.

At the house, you can't see the water or the boardwalks that well because of the two giant trees in the backyard, but I see my husband peeking out from the basement patio to watch.

Dad rounds on me and I wait for him to blow up, but he doesn't.

"You need to give Kyle and Miley custody of Micah." He says.

Confusion hits first, and then shock.

"Wait, what?" I ask.

"You need to give Kyle and Miley custody of Micah." He repeats.

"Dad, you just went homeless fighting for custody." I say.

"I was fighting for custody over me and your mother, because everyone knows I'm the better choice." He says. "But Micah deserves to have a loving mother and a loving father. Miley and Kyle can't have kids and it doesn't take a blind person to realize how much they love Micah and how much Micah loves them. You could see from the look on both of their faces that they want kids."

"So you want me to give them custody?" I ask slowly.

"Yes."

"But I want custody." I say.

"I know kid." He whispers. "And so do I, but you're starting your own family and you never planned to have to raise your brother."

"I don't mind."

"But Micah minds."

We're both quiet, and I look down.

"But what if they move away?"

"You and Danny can come see him when I use my visitation rights."

"You're willing to just give him up like that?" I mumble.

"Grace," Dad sighs slowly. "This is what he wants."

The thought of letting Micah leave me hurt my heart, but Danny and I are having a new baby soon and I don't want him to feel like we don't care. I'm sure all of our focus will be on Emily, and Micah might start to feel a little left out. He's been considering Kyle and Miley his parents, and every child deserves a set of loving parents.

"Let me go talk to Danny." I mumble sadly.

I waddle back across the boardwalk and up the small slope.

I see movement under the stairs and then silence, so with a roll of of eyes, I maneuver around the stairs and see my husband crouched behind a bush in a white shirt, thinking he's being slick at watching us.

"You know when you used to do that as a kid, it was me you were doing it with." I gesture to his hiding spot. "You're not slick."

He huffs and stands up.

"What did he say to you?"

I look down.

"He told me to give custody to Kyle and Miley."

"Why?" He asks.

"Because it's what Micah wants."

"Micah is five years old. He doesn't know what he wants. I don't want him to leave. He's my little buddy. He watches sports with me. I have been teaching him football because I recorded all the games."

"I don't want him to leave either, Danny, but my Dad thinks we should give custody of Kyle and Miley, and honestly baby, I kind of agree with him."

Danny kicks at a rock, frowning.

"Why?" He asks.

"Because every child deserves to have a loving set of parents."

"We can be his loving set of parents though!" Danny exclaims.

"Sweetheart, in Micah's mind, we will never be his parents. He already considers Kyle and Miley his parents."

Danny hangs his head.

"Fine." He says finally. "But only because it's what Micah wants."

He turn around and walks back into the basement.

"Wait." I say, rushing after him. He turns around to face me. "Promise me that we won't have to deal with this with Emily and whatever kids we have after her." I whisper. "Promise me we're going to be good parents, because I can't bring a baby into the world knowing there's a chance I could have to give her up."

His eyes soften and he walks back over to me, putting his hands on my face.

"Sweetheart, we will never have to even think of giving up our little girl, and whatever siblings we make for her. We're going to love her and cherish her and be the best parents we can possibly be for her."

"Do you promise?" I whisper.

"I promise." He nods. "And if somebody tries to take her from us...we run to another country."

*****

Asking Kyle and Miley if they still wanted custody of Micah was one of the hardest things I have ever had to do.

But the look on their faces when I asked, that sheer joy, that was enough for me. Dad was standing right there when I asked, along with Danny and

Caleb and Beatrice, and everyone just kind of looked at Dad, and he said that Micah deserves to be happy.

No matter how much it hurts me to let him go, it feels right.

So now that we're back in the room with Micah, I clear my throat.

"Hey Micah?"

He looks up from his book where he's sounding out the words with Miley.

"Yes?"

Ask the question. Just do it.

"What do you think about going to live with Kyle and Miley...forever?"

He hesitates.

"Do you and Danny not want me anymore?" He asks quietly.

"Bud, your sister and I will always want you around." Danny says. "But if you live with Kyle and Miley, you could have a Mom and a Dad."

Micah hesitates.

"But what about my real Dad?" He asks.

"He would still be your Dad too." Kyle says. "You could have two Dad's."

"Well would you still be my big sister?" Micah asks.

"Of course she would." Miley says. "And you can come see her whenever you want."

"But will I be Emily's uncle?"

"Yes, of course." I say.

He hesitates.

"So I'm being adopted?"

"If you want." Danny says quietly.

Micah looks down at his book and then at Miley, and then at Kyle.

"Okay, can we do that? I want to do that." He says.

Danny puts his hands on my shoulders.

"I'll start researching how to go about doing this." I mumble, pushing up from the table.

*****

I have to be up at 5:30AM every day this week and this daylight savings could not have come at the worst time

~Sam

Chapter Fifteen: 11:52PM

Everyone is staring at me.

They're like hungry vultures waiting for me to flinch, hoping for some sort of pain.

The fact that they're hoping I'm in pain is bad enough.

I'm starving.

I sigh and stand up, my hand on my belly, which is bigger than it has ever been my whole life.

The moment I stand, Danny and Beatrice get up too.

"Where are you going?" Danny asks.

"I'm going to eat."

I've been getting braxton hicks for about two weeks, which is when my stomach gets hard and it feels like I have period cramps. It's not too bad but sometimes it does make me cringe. Today though, they hurt more than they have recently, because today is Saturday, June twenty first.

Today is my due date.

Megan and Abby are here, Miley and Kyle are here with Micah, my Dad is here because we haven't found him an apartment yet. Beatrice and Caleb are still staying with us for another month or two. My Dad's parents are here, and the rest of the family is on standby, waiting for a message that I'm in labor.

"Well what are you making? Let me get it for you."

"No." I reply, walking into the kitchen.

Everyone always says to walk, so I'm getting up.

Emily is supposed to come today, so I'm making sure I have her today.

I make two hot pockets and walk around the living room as I eat them.

"You're seriously not in any pain?" Abby asks impatiently.

I feel another braxton hick.

"I'm getting braxton hicks." I say. I've noticed that each time I get them, they hurt worse, but I'm expecting to want to cry from the pain and I'm nowhere near that.

Everyone seems to be impatient but there's nobody more impatient than I am, so I go into the bathroom and brush my teeth.

"I need to talk to you." I lie to Danny. "Can you come here?"

He nods and follows me upstairs.

I take my time getting up the stairs because I have a giant belly and I'm afraid to slip and fall on Emily.

I go into our bedroom and shut the door behind him.

"Yes?" He asks.

"I need you to shave my vagina."

"What?" He starts laughing.

"I can't do it." I say. "I can't see down there, but you can do it."

"Grace..."

"Please?"

"Alright." He sighs.

I lock the bedroom door and sprawl out on the floor.

He helps me get my pants down, shaking his head at me.

"I can't believe I'm doing this." He mutters.

"Well you didn't really try to fight it that much."

"Oh, and after you're done, we're going to have sex, because sex can apparently make me go into labor."

*****

We were upstairs for two hours, and the braxton hicks are getting bad enough to make me clench my jaw when they come now, so I don't know if they're braxton hicks anymore.

I keep walking around the living room, impatient for more contractions.

The doctor said she doesn't want to induce me unless I get a week past my due date.

A full week.

But I'm not going a week past. I refuse.

"We should go to the mall." I say. "Take a nice long walk. We can go to Gymboree, you know how much I love that store." I say to Danny.

"We're not going to the mall." He sighs.

"Fine. Can you go to the basement and get my bouncy ball thing?" I ask.

He stands up and goes downstairs.

After a minute, he comes back with my blue big bouncy ball. I take it and sit down on it, and I start to bounce.

I really want some chips though, so I get off the ball and go get a bag of ruffles sour cream and onion, and I start bouncing again, snacking on my chips.

Everyone just sits there on their phones or watching me.

Danny is the one that's watching me though, sitting up wringing his hands together anxiously.

"You don't have any contractions?" He asks finally.

I shrug.

"I'm not sure."

But right as I say it, I get this dull ache in my lower back, followed by this feeling of sheer agony starting from the top of uterus to the bottom. I stop bouncing and the chips fall from my hands, screwing my eyes shut. I curl the fabric of my sweatpants into my hand and wait for it to pass.

It's feels like a glorified period cramp, but it's a million times worse. It's a pain so bad that I forget to breathe.

After what feels like minutes, the pain slowly fades away.

When I open my eyes, everyone in the room is staring at me.

"That was a contraction." I say. I pick my chip bag up with my foot and start bouncing again.

"I'm calling the doctor." He says.

"Danny, it was one contraction." I remind him.

"I don't care. I'm just going to call her and tell her it's starting."

"Alright, fine."

I ditch the ball and walk to the kitchen to put my chips back, and then I start walking around the house.

After a few minutes, Danny walks back into the living room.

"She said to go to the hospital if you get contractions every five minutes, each of them lasting a full minute, and they have been that way for an hour." He pauses. "And she also said to go straight to the hospital if your water breaks."

"Let's go on a really long walk around the neighborhood."

He opens his mouth to argue, but I'm really heading for the door.

I hear him sigh and follow me.

*****

It took him an hour to convince me to go back home. I had a lot of contractions on the walk, and when I get back in the house, I'm sweating from the pain. I have Danny help me up the stairs and I put on a sports bra and a pair of his basketball shorts, and now I'm back on the bouncy ball.

Another contraction hits.

"Grace, I know it hurts honey but you need to remember to breathe." Beatrice says. I force myself to take a deep breath mid contraction, and I keep trying to control my breathing, but this one is the worst one yet, and it's strong enough to make my whimper.

"I want to get drugged right now." I say when it's over.

"I know." Danny says. "But we can't go until your contractions are give minutes apart, lasting a full minute, for an hour straight."

I move so the ball is right in front of Danny, and he keeps his hands on my thighs while I bounce. I grasp both of his hands and hold on, bouncing up and down.

I feel another contraction coming and I stop bouncing.

I take a deep breath through my nose and blow it out of my mouth the whole time I'm having contractions, and each time they hurt worse and worse.

"We need to make sure the hospital bag is packed. And the diaper bag. And the car seat needs to be taken out of the back of the Jeep and clipped into the base. And the sucker thing needs to be in the diaper bag too, because if I have her in the car we need to suck all the stuff out of her mouth so she doesn't choke. Oh god, another one is coming, here we go again."

I squeeze Danny's hands this time and keep breathing. The pain slowly fades after about thirty seconds, and I go back to bouncing.

"What can I do?" Danny asks when it passes. He starts rubbing my arm.

"I need some ice. It's hot in here."

I'm actually sweating.

"Okay." He says. "Do you want a drink?"

"I just want crushed ice please." I mumble.

"Okay." He squeezes my shoulder and gets up.

I hear the ice machine come on and a moment later he comes back with a cup of ice and a spoon, and he sits back down behind me.

I scoop some ice into my mouth and start chewing it, and I can feel Emily shifting her feet inside of me, but she isn't moving much during the contractions.

Another one starts and I squeeze Danny's hand again, breathing heavily.

"God, how is it happening this fast?" I mumble.

"This is how it was you're your mother." Dad says. "For both you and Micah. And if your labor is anything like hers, you're going to get to the hospital at ten centimeters and the baby will be in your arms within the hour."

Wonderful. Just great.

"Somebody might want to start timing them." I mumble, rubbing my belly.

"I'll do it." Beatrice stands up and walks over to me, sitting down on the new coffee table.

After a few minutes of me bouncing, another contraction hits and I watch Beatrice's breathing to remind myself to breathe, too.

When it's over, I look at her.

"It was twenty seconds sweetie. We're going to be here a while."

*****

I bounced for three hours before I got up and started walking around again, but the contractions I'm having now make the first one feel like nothing.

I feel another one hit and I grasp the back of the couch, dropping my forehead against it. I feel Danny's hand on my back.

"Oh my god, it hurts so bad." I whimper.

"I know baby, I know." Danny says. It's around nine now and I've been having contractions since about ten this morning, which means I've been in labor for eleven hours.

I moan softly in pain, and after what feels like hours, it slowly fades.

"That one was a minute long. I have the timer going for the time it takes for the next one to start." She says.

"Do you want more ice?" Danny asks.

"I want the pain to stop." I mumble.

"I know princess, I know." He says.

I stand up straight and start walking around again.

After a few minutes, the next one starts.

"Oh god." I groan. "Oh my god, oh my god, make it stop."

I'm squeezing Danny's hand so hard, I'm worried I might break it, but he doesn't seem to mind.

After an eternity, it stops.

"It was five minutes apart and that one was a minute long also." Beatrice says.

"Oh thank god." I mumble. "Can we go now?" I ask Danny.

"We can't baby, it has to keep going for an hour."

I turn around and bury my head in his chest.

"It'll be over soon." He murmurs.

"I need to go pee." I mumble.

"Okay, come on."

He walks with me to the bathroom and we're in and out.

The second we reach the living room, another one starts and I clutch onto Danny to stay upright. I feel him pulling my sweaty hair off of my neck while I squeeze his hand as hard as I can.

When it ends, I look at Beatrice.

"It was a minute long, five minutes apart." She says gently.

"This is good." Danny says, rubbing my back. "We can go to the hospital soon and get the epidural."

*****

The hour slowly trickled past and each contraction was worse than the last, and the last one I had, I was full fletched crying.

"That marks the hour." Beatrice says.

"Okay, let's go now." Danny says.

Caleb grabs the hospital bag and the diaper bag.

"Do we have everything?" I whimper.

"Every we need is in the bag." Danny says. He helps me down the basement stairs and right when we reach my Jeep, I rest my hands against the door and keel forward as another one hits.

"I can't do it, I can't do it." I whimper. "Oh my god, it hurts so bad."

"You can do it." Danny says. "You're doing excellent baby. It'll be over soon."

When it passes, he puts me in the car.

"That was four minutes apart. We need to go now." Beatrice urges.

Caleb puts the bags in the back seat and everyone takes their own cars. Danny helps me into ours and I prepare myself for the pain I'm about to endure.

The entire car ride was spent with me clutching onto the handle and crying from pain every few minutes and Danny talking to my doctor on the phone who told him she was on her way right now.

When we reach the emergency room, Danny parks the car and grabs the bags, walking me inside. I guess my doctor lives right by the hospital, because she's already waiting.

"Let's get you into a wheelchair." She says. "And into the delivery room as fast as possible."

She grabs a wheelchair by the door and Danny helps me into it, walking next to me as we get on the elevator. I feel another contraction and I clench Danny's hand, whimpering from the pain.

"I don't want to do this." I look at him. "I can't do this. It hurts so much. I can't do this."

"You can do this baby, you're doing so great already."

"Gracelyn," my doctor moves in front of me when we get in the elevator. "The contractions are the worst of it honey."

"Okay, but I want drugs. I want all the drugs you can give me."

"We will give you an epidural." She says.

"Yes. I want it right away. The second you can drug me, I want it. I'm not kidding. Numb me up, cut me open, I don't care, just make the pain stop."

The elevator dings on the labor and delivery floor and I she starts pushing me down the hall. She uses her badge to get in, already dressed in her pink scrubs, and another contraction starts and I cling to my husband.

When we reach the delivery room. There's a few nurses in here, a plastic crib, and I'm scared. I'm terrified.

They help me into the hospital gown and they make Danny put something on the front of his clothes, and then they help me into the bed.

"I don't want any other family coming in here until after she's born." I tell the nurses as one of them puts an IV in my right hand. "Only hospital staff, okay?"

"Okay." My doctor says.

"We'll make sure nobody else comes in."

Another contraction hits and I cling to my husband and his hands are pulling my sweaty hair off of my neck.

"I can't do this. I don't want to be a Mom anymore. I just want it to stop." I whimper.

"Well it's a little bit late for that honey." Danny says.

They set me up with some medicine.

"So give me the epidural." I tell my doctor. "Where the anesthesiologist?"

She pushes my legs apart and hesitates.

"What?" I demand. "Why do you look like that? What's wrong?"

"Grace, I don't want you to panic, but I can see your baby's head."

Oh my god.

"Do you can't drug me?" I whisper.

"I can't drug you." She says. "Somebody get the nursery on the phone and tell them we need a room ready." She orders. "Now all I need you to do is remember to breathe as you push. If you remember to breathe, you can make this be much, much shorter."

"Okay." I whisper, grasping Danny's hand.

"Get ready to cut the cord." She tells Danny. I feel another contraction coming and nurses are standing around the bed ready for anything. One is across the room on a phone, and I realize this is happening. I'm giving birth, and I'm doing it without any drugs.

"Okay Grace, I want you to give me a big push."

I take a deep breath and push as hard as I can, tears are streaming down my face from the pain, and I'm groaning and Danny is reminding me to breathe and telling me how good I'm doing.

"Okay, stop." My doctor says. "Catch your breath."

I take the time to take a few deep breaths.

"Now go."

I push again and it hurts so bad. After a few seconds, I'm told to stop again, and this continues over the next hour.

"I can't do it anymore." I gasp. "I can't. I can't. Just-just cut me open!"

I have sweat dripping down my body and my face is wet with tears.

"You're almost there." Danny says.

"Just one more push. One more really big push." Dr. Edwards says. "Can you give me one more push?"

I take a deep breath and start to push, crying and screaming and clutching Danny's hand.

"Okay, stop." Dr. Edwards says. There is silence for a moment, and then a loud cry fills the room and I feel chills running through my entire body.

"I did it?!" I gasp.

"You did it." Danny laughs, and he has tears in his eyes.

"Come cut the cord." Dr. Edwards tells Danny.

I see a little tiny baby in Dr. Edwards arms covered in gunk and and I start laughing, because that's our baby girl.

The cord gets clamped and Danny cuts it.

"I want to hold her." I sniffle, holding my arms out. She's screaming, but I've never been more happy.

Dr. Edwards hands her to me, and she's so incredible.

"Oh my god." I say, tears gushing down my cheeks. "She's so beautiful."

The nurse comes up with the sucker thing and starts sucking gunk from her mouth and nose. Dr. Edwards is tending to me down below.

"Can I take her to clean her up?" The nurse asks.

"Yes." I sniffle. She carefully takes my little baby away from me, and I turn to Danny.

"Go with her."

He kisses my temple and walks away.

Dr. Edwards helps me into a pair of panties and they clean up the bed.

I watch the nurse from across the room as she washes Emily and checks her joints, and after weighing her and measuring her, she comes back with a clean baby who now is wearing a diaper is is swaddled in the blue and pink and white striped hospital blanket.

She hands her back to me and I take her, gently pulling the blanket down so I can see her. Danny moves next to me and he took off the gown thing they made him wear.

The nurses are moving around the room doing what they have to.

"Are you okay?" Danny asks me as I look down at Emily. "How do you feel?"

"I'm a little sore but okay." I murmur.

Emily is beautiful. She's not screaming anymore. She has a head of light blonde hair. Her nose is identical to mine. She has my lips too, and my eyes, and my face shape. She looks just like me, but she has Danny's ears. I gently reach out to brush my fingertips across her soft cheek.

"She's beautiful." I whisper, turning to look at Danny. He smiles and kisses me.

"We did good baby, we did good." He says. "You did really good. I can't imagine going through what you just did."

I look down at our little girl and smile.

"It was worth it."

"She is six pounds, four ounces, and eighteen inches long." My doctor says. "And she is beautiful and healthy."

I laugh softly with sheer joy.

"She looks just like her Momma." Danny murmurs.

"What's her name?" A nurse asks, holding a card in her hand.

"Her name is Emily." I whisper.

Danny was right, Mariposa wouldn't have fit. Emily, however, is a perfect name for her.

"The nurse changes one of my IV bags.

"This is just medicine to help your uterus contract back to it's original size." She says. "And congratulations."

"Thank you." I whisper.

My doctor walks back over to us after writing in her chart.

"She was born at 11:52." She laughs. "June twenty first."

I smile.

"Also, you're very lucky you didn't need any stitches."

I just smile and look back at Emily.

"Now I'm going to go. The nurses will help you. I'll be back in the morning to check on you. If you need me, call me."

"Thank you so much, Dr. Edwards, and then you for helping me not giving up." I laugh. "It was definitely worth all the pain."

"Oh, it always is." She smiles.

"Thank you." Danny says sincerely. "For keeping my girls safe."

"It was my pleasure."

With that, she leaves.

After a few minutes, Emily opens her eyes and starts to fuss.

"Are you planning on nursing?" One of the nurses asks me. The rest of them leave the room.

"Yes." I say, bouncing her as she cries.

"You might want to feed her now."

"Um, okay." I say nervously. "I don't know how."

"I know, it's okay." She laughs. "You just swap sides for each feeding. So you can start with whatever side."

Her head is on my left side, so I decide I'll start there.

She unbuttons the left shoulder on my hospital gown.

"You might want to take off your sports bra. It'll be easier." She says.

"Okay."

I'm kind of nervous for this, but I need somebody to take her from me.

"I want her." Danny says.

I hold her out for him to grasp, and he carefully takes her from my arms. She's still crying to be fed. I pull the hospital gown off and remove my sports bra, and then I put the gown back on.

Danny hands her back to me with a smile, and I pull the gown down to expose my breast.

"Now you want to squeeze to make sure your milk is coming out." She says.

With my other hand, I reach over and squeeze my breast, and I see a little white droplet coming out.

"Now as you go to feed her, you hold the nipple, but hold it so your fingers are about two inches apart so they're not in her way."

I do as she says.

"Now guide her mouth to your nipple. Babies are born knowing how to suck, but now how to latch."

"Um, she's not opening her mouth." I mumble.

"So rub your nipple on her lips." She says."And aim kind of her upper lip, not the middle.

I do what she says and a moment later, Emily grasps on with her mouth and starts to suck.

"Is it right?" I ask.

The nurse leans over to see.

"It looks right. She's not making any sounds."

"Okay. Thank you."

"You're welcome. My name is Caroline. If you need help, just ask somebody at the desk. I'll be back in about fifteen minutes to check on you, and when she's done, we're going to go ahead and move you to the nursery floor."

"Thank you." I say.

"You're welcome."

She walks out, leaving me alone with Danny and Emily.

My husband pulls up a chair.

"What does it feel like?" He asks.

"It feels like she's sucking on my nipple." I laugh.

He smiles, and I swear this is one of the best days of my life.

*****

I cried, big surprise there

~Sam

Chapter Sixteen: Hose

Chapter Sixteen: Hose

I feel my shoulder being gently shaken, causing me to force my eyes open. My husband stands over me. Emily is fast asleep on my chest and somebody is knocking on the hospital door.

"Everyone really wanted to come in to see you guys." He whispers. "And they've been waiting for hours."

I blink a few times and put my hand on Emily's head, sitting up. I carefully shift her so I'm cradling her, and she doesn't stir at all.

"Do you want me to ask them to come in the morning?"

"No, it's okay." I murmur. "What time is it?"

"It's a little after two." He whispers.

I nursed her and then gave her to Danny to burp her and once he was done holding her, I took her back and passed out. I'm so physically drained, I could sleep on anything.

"You can let them in." I murmur.

"Okay." He kisses my head and walks over to the door, pulling it open.

Our relatives are here, and Danny's Nana and Papa are here now too. I tasked Beatrice with sending the news, so they must have come to the hospital when they got the call.

Everyone slowly files into the room with smiles. They all look tired as they creep closer to peek at Emily.

"How are you feeling?" Caleb asks me.

"I'm tired." I say.

Micah is still awake, dragging his feet as he walks. His eyes are droopy.

"We were going to take him home but he begged to stay to see the baby." Miley whispers.

"How about you three go first then?" Danny suggests. "So you can get him into bed."

"Yes, if we could, that'd be great." Kyle says.

"Can I hold her?" Micah asks me.

"Sure, but go wash your hands. All of you."

Everyone forms a line to the sink and Micah goes first, and then he walks over to the bed and climbs up. I sit up, wincing slightly at the pain.

"Do you need anything?" Danny asks me. "Medicine? Water?"

"I'm okay." I murmur. "Thank you."

He just squeezes my shoulder in response.

I have Micah sit back close to me and I shift so I'm holding Emily by her head and her butt. I lift her over his head until she's in front of him and

Danny helps to adjust his arms so he's holding her, but I'm actually the one holding her.

Miley takes the picture and we both smile at the camera.

After a moment longer, Micah sighs.

"She's not doing anything."

"She's a baby buddy. Babies don't do anything until they get older." Kyle says.

"I want to be done please." He says.

I lift her out of his arms and he climbs off the bed.

Miley rubs her hands together and holds her arms out, and I carefully pass her to her, my hand lingering on her head until I'm sure she's got her.

She takes the baby and looks down at her.

"God, she looks just like you, Grace." She says.

"She's adorable." Danny smiles.

"You're not upset that she doesn't look a lot like you?" Kyle asks.

"Not really. I know she's mine." He laughs. I lean over and rest my head against his side.

After a few minutes, she passes her to Kyle.

"I call dibs next." Beatrice says suddenly, causing all of us to look at her.

"I want dibs after her." Caleb says.

"I want dibs after Caleb." Abby says at the same time that Mega says "I'm after him then."

"Uh, I said it first." Abby says.

"No you didn't." Megan argues.

"Yes I did."

"Did not."

"Did too."

"Grace!" They say in sync, turning to look at me.

"My Dad goes before both of you." I say. "And then I'll pick."

The arguing stops, and after another moment, Kyle hands Emily to Beatrice.

"Oh my." She whispers. "She looks exactly like you, Grace. I feel like I'm holding you all over again."

"She has Danny's ears though." Caleb says.

"Whats her measurements?" Dad asks.

"Six pounds, four ounces, eighteen inches." I yawn. "She was born at 11:52."

"That's creepy." Dad says.

"Why?" I frown.

"That's your measurements too."

"She's going to look just like you." Danny says. "I'm going to be fending off boys by the time she's out of diapers."

I roll my eyes.

After a few minutes, Caleb gets impatient and walks over to his wife, gently taking Emily.

"I wasn't done." Beatrice mutters.

"Well you are now."

"Guys, it's way too late to be salty." I mutter.

After a few minutes, Dad walks up to Caleb and does the same thing he just did to Beatrice.

"Wow." Dad says. "The resemblance is remarkable. If I had Alzheimer's, I would think this is you."

She's starting to wake up now, and the nurse told me to feed her every two hours and it's getting close to that time again.

After about another minute of Dad holding her, she starts to cry. She probably needs a diaper change. Danny hands me the diaper bag before I can ask him for it, and I lie her down in front of me.

She probably needs to put on some type of clothes because she's only in her diaper. I carefully undo the swaddle to reveal her bare chest, and she's so cute. Her eyes are wide open and she's staring right at me. Everyone creeps closer to watch, and the line on her diaper is blue but the bottom is yellow, so she peed.

I get the wipes and a fresh diaper, and Danny hands me clothes for her. It's a white long sleeve footed pajama set. There are tiny dots that are small strawberries, and the feet of the pajamas are strawberries.

I carefully undo her diaper and wipe her up, and then I put a new diaper on and unzip the outfit.

I lie her down and put her feet in the spots, and then her arms, and I zip it back up.

"Megan can hold her." I say, handing the dirty diaper to Danny, who throws it out.

I hand her off to Megan, but the moment she's out of my arms, she starts to fuss again.

Megan hesitates.

"Never mind, I think she's hungry." I mumble.

Danny hands me the cover up and I do the same thing I did on my left side on the right. Her fussing stops when she latches on and I rest back, sighing.

Beatrice was right. Trying to run across the house every time she wakes up is going to be really annoying.

"I think we're going to leave." Kyle says after a minute. "Get Micah to bed and stuff."

"Alright." I murmur.

"We'll probably come back in the morning." Miley says. She leans down to hug me and waves to Danny and everyone else, and then they leave with Micah.

After a few minutes, there's a soft knock on the door and the nurse sticks her head in.

"How are we doing?" She asks. She talks loudly and it doesn't seem to bother Emily.

"Good. Tired." I smile softly.

"Do you want me to take Emily to the nursery so you guys can get some sleep?" She asks.

I told Danny when I first got pregnant that the baby will not leave our sight until we're home. I watched switched at birth in college and I want to raise the baby that I created.

"No, we're okay."

"Are you sure?" She asks.

"I'm sure."

All it takes is them switching the cribs and I might never find out again.

Danny nods in agreement with me.

"Alrighty then. How's baby doing?"

"She's okay. When can we leave?"

"Grace, you've been here a couple of hours." Dad says.

"Yeah, the baby is out and I want to go home."

I hate sleeping without Danny next to me, and I have since around the time we started dating. It gives me anxiety being alone, even if I know he's in the room. If I can't physically reach over and touch him, I get nervous.

"Hopefully sometime tomorrow, but Dr. Edwards might want you guys to stay until Monday. We have to put the drops in Emily's eyes, check her hearing..." she trails off.

"Well does Emily have a low birth weight?" I ask, even though I know the answer.

"No." She says.

"And she's not showing any signs of problems. Can't you discharge us at night? We can run through everything tomorrow and then you can send us on our way."

"Unfortunately, I don't get to decide these things. You can hash it out with Dr. Edwards."

Dr. Edwards knows I'm stubborn when it comes to certain things. She's been my doctor since day one.

"Alright. Hey, don't you have one of those wire things you can put on her ankle?" I ask.

"What is that for?" Danny asks.

"It's so if somebody takes her near an exit, the doors lock in the entire hospital." I reply.

"Why do you want one of those?" Danny asks.

"Well I don't want Mom showing up trying to steal her."

"Grace, she's not showing up. She doesn't even know where you live." Dad says.

"Well she could find out. You did, didn't you?"

"Yeah..." he trails off.

"Exactly." I look at the nurse. "Do you have one?"

"I can get one." She nods.

"Thank you." I say. "And can you like...write on something and stick it on the door that the baby doesn't leave the room unless my husband or myself is with her?"

"Yes, I'll do that too."

"Thank you." I say. "Can I get up? I'm tired of sitting, and I have to pee."

"Sure."

I sit up fully.

"Not yet." She laughs nervously. "You can't get up with the baby."

"Why not?" I ask.

"Grace, you could pass out or something." Danny says. "Just wait until you're done feeding her."

"Alright." I mutter.

"Let me go get the ankle thing and write the sign on the door." The nurse says.

"Thank you."

"You're welcome." she walks out.

I feel Emily detach her mouth and I pull her off of my breast.

The second she's free, Danny reaches out and takes her from me.

"It's my turn." He says.

"Actually, I didn't get a turn." Abby grumbles.

"Megan got her for literally a second. Megan gets her after she's burped and then you can have her." I tell Abby.

"Alright."

Danny holds Emily so she's upside down on his arm and he has her face in his hands. Her starts burping her.

"Are we going to pay for professional pictures?" I ask Danny.

"Yes." He says. "I want to be one of those Dad's that has a picture of my kid in my wallet so when I open it up to pay and there's a girl that likes me, I can brag about my daughter with my visibly ringed left hand. And I want a framed picture of her in the house somewhere, maybe above the bed."

"We're not putting a picture of her above the bed."

"Why? That wall is bare."

"Because we have sex in the bed, and I don't want to look up and see my daughters face staring back at me."

He hesitates.

"Good point."

"I will find somewhere for her picture, but it's not going in our room."

"Okay, but can we still-"

I hear a loud liquid farting sound omit from our daughter, and then she burps, dropping spit up all over the floor.

"Look at that." Danny grins. "How cute!"

She burps her for a few more seconds, and then he stops and lies her down on my bed.

"Can I change her?" He asks me.

"She's not only my baby Danny. You can do whatever you want. She's just as much mine as she is yours."

At that, he grins and looks down at Emily, who is staring right up at him with wide brown eyes.

"I'm the one that has been talking to you every day since before you could hear me." He informs her. She looks mesmerized by his voice, staring up at him with wide eyes.

He grabs the diaper bag off the floor, keeping one hand on her belly, and he sets the bag down on the bed. He unzips her star berry pajamas.

"She's so cute. Look at her." Danny says.

"I know." I smile.

This interaction is so cute. I love seeing him be a Dad.

He pulls her little legs out of the pajamas and pushes them up under her back. She just keeps staring at him.

When he undoes the diaper, we both wrinkle our noses, because the first baby poop is known to be the grossest, and Emily's is jet black and it looks like paint.

"Oh, that's disgusting." Danny mutters. "Where do I even start with this?"

"I don't know. Wing it."

He grabs a wipe and just stares at the mess.

I push the blankets off of my lap.

"Are you getting up?" He asks.

"Yes."

He drops the wipe on the bed and keeps one hand on Emily and uses the other to help me out of bed.

I take a second to just stand, and when I'm sure I'm not dizzy, I move to stand next to him.

Emily is staring at both of us now, and she's so cute I can't handle it.

After a moment, she starts to pee, completely exposed, and it's not like a gentle trickle, it's like a hose, shooting both of us in the face.

I screech and Danny yelps. I move out of the way of the stream and wipe her urine off my face with the hospital gown, but she's still shooting Danny, so I use my hand to stop the spray, completely coating her belly in pee.

Our whole family is roaring in laughter as my husband removes his shirt to wipe his face, and then mine.

We both look down at our daughter who is still staring at us, adorable as ever.

I look at my husband who has damp hair stuck to his forehead.

"We need to make sure to keep the diaper closed." I mumble.

He hesitates, looking at me, back at Emily, and back at me, and then he starts laughing and I do too, until we're both standing there shaking with silent laughter.

After a moment, Emily starts to scream.

"Okay," I snort, hitting my husbands arm. "We need to tend to the child."

He grabs the wipe and starts to clean her up, still laughing as he does it. I fold up the diaper and he puts a new one on, checking to make sure it's not too tight.

Her strawberry pajamas have pee on them, so he pulls her arms out. I get another pair of pajamas from the diaper bag, and this one is pink with white spots and has an elephant on the side.

He swaps them out and uses a wipe to clean pee off of her, and then he zips her back up.

"Yeah, we should probably take a shower. Am I allowed to shower?"

"Ask the nurse." Danny says, lifting Emily up.

Megan sticks her hands out for her, and I honestly forgot everyone was there.

Danny hands Emily to her.

"Let me go find the nurse." He says, tossing his shirt in the grocery bag.

He walks out in just his jeans and I guess the nurse is right outside the door.

After a minute, he comes back.

"She said you can shower if somebody watches over you to make sure you don't pass out."

"Well you can just shower with me." I yawn.

"Okay." He says. He grabs the hospital bag. "Do you want a new one of those?" He points to the hospital gown I'm wearing.

"No, I want a tank top and pajama pants. Something loose and thin."

He digs through the bag and gets his stuff, and he pulls out one of my tank tops and then shrugs and hands the bag to me.

I get out my blue thin pajama pants, a nursing bra, and a fresh pair of panties, along with a pair of new panties.

"Grace." Danny says suddenly. When I look at him, his face is pale. "You have blood running down your leg."

*****

I am so tired I took a nap and I'm still exhausted, I can't wait until Friday

~Sam

Chapter Seventeen: Incompetence

Chapter Seventeen: Incompetence

Danny

I sit in the waiting room. The plastic crib sits in front of me and Emily is sleeping peacefully. I'm pulling the crib back and forth.

The blood was gushing down her leg into a puddle on the floor, and I knew her period would start back up, but we were told multiple times that it's just like a period after you give birth, and a normal period doesn't run down your leg like that. The moment I saw the blood, I knew she was hemorrhaging.

And now I've never been more scared in my life.

The moment everyone saw the blood, everything turned to chaos. Nurses were running in and out of the room, telling us to get out. Grace was pleading with me not to let Emmy out of my sight, and I was begging her to be okay, trying to go back to stay with her. Megan was clinging to Emily, who was screaming, and my Mom was grabbing the hospital bags, and Dad was pulling me from the room.

And now I'm sitting in the waiting room, one hand pushing the crib back and forth and the other resting on my forehead.

I don't do this well. I've never done well with Grace being in pain. When Grace and I were babies, she was waking around and tripped and slammed her forehead on the corner of a shelf and she was screaming, and because she was crying, my Mom told me I started crying. I remember standing in the bathroom every time she skinned her knee when we were playing outside and I would hold her hand as her Mom or Dad or one of my parents poured peroxide on her hand.

The first time her Mom raised her hand to her, I cried when we hung up the phone because I had a gut feeling it was going to get worse. When she choked her, I cried again, right in front of Grace on camera. Seeing her in any pain at all makes my body physically hurt, but knowing she's bleeding a lot and there's nothing I can do about it...it makes it unbearable.

I'm trying my hardest not to cry in front of everyone.

I hardly ever cry. There is one thing in this world I cry over, and that's Grace. Every single time. I cried today because Emily was born, and the time before that was probably when she told me she was pregnant, or maybe the first ultrasound. I don't know. I only cry in situations that involve my wife and daughter.

And I'm scared. I'm so scared. My hands are clamming and I'm trying not to start shaking, because what if something is really, really wrong?

I don't want to even think about what's going to happen to me if she doesn't come out of this alive. The thought alone makes me sick. I can't think about it. I literally can't. I'll start crying.

Mom reaches over to rub my back.

What if I made her laugh from when Emmy peed? What if it's all my fault?

I hear footsteps.

"I just got the call." Kyle says breathlessly. "What the hell happened? She was fine!"

She was fine. She was perfectly fine. She was smiling and happy.

Without a word, I push the plastic crib to my Mom and stand up, walking out without a word.

"Where are you going?" Mom calls, but I just keep walking.

I can't breathe in that sterile hospital. I need to think.

I take the stairs instead of the elevator, rushing outside when I reach the first floor. The ground is soaked so I know it rained.

I just keep walking until I reach the Jeep, and I feel like I'm being suffocated with emotions. I slide down the side of the Jeep until I'm crouching with my back against the sleek black door. I bury my head in my hands, and start crying.

What the fuck. How could this happen? She was fine? She was okay. She was up and walking and talking and laughing with that beautiful smile and seeing her nurse our baby and watching her dress her and just be a Momma...that was the most incredible sight of my life, and then I look down and there was just...blood. So much blood.

She was pale. Did she know she was bleeding? I don't think she did, because after she saw the blood, she looks up at me, and that look in her eye, that sheer fear...it was enough to rip my heart out.

What if she bled out? What if she passed out and she never wakes up again?

I hear footsteps and I need to compose myself, but I can't.

My princess. My baby. My Gracie.

I've lived and breathed that woman for sixteen years.

Sixteen years of me thinking about her, and only her.

"Do you want to talk about it?" I hear my Dad ask. I look up and see him standing next to the taillight, his hands stuffed in his pockets.

"Go away. I'm crying."

"So?" He asks. "I've seen you cry, and I've seen you cry over Grace almost every time I've seen you cry."

He walks closer to me and sits down on the ground next to me.

"Dad, is she going to die?" I whisper, frantically spinning the wedding ring around and around my finger.

"She's going to be fine." Dad says calmly. "Grace has been through a lot more than losing a little bit of blood. She's the strongest woman I've ever met in my entire life."

"I'm scared." I whisper. "I'm so scared. What if something is really, really wrong? What if I have to raise Emily alone?"

"You don't." Dad says. "Grace is going to be fine. Dr. Edwards is really good and she came right back. Everything is going to be fine bud. You need to be strong, not just for your daughter, but for your wife."

I sniffle and nod, wiping my eyes.

"She's gonna be fine." Dad repeats. "It's probably taking so long so she can question the doctors about everything they're doing."

I sniffle and smile slightly, nodding.

"I mean, she's one of the most bossiest people I've ever known." He adds.

I laugh a little, nodding some more.

"Yeah, she really is. She's great." I wring my hands together.

"Let's go inside. My ass is soaked." He stands up off the wet pavement and offers me his hand. I take it and he pulls me to my feet.

I wipe my face with my hand and decide I don't care if everyone knows I was crying.

He walks with me back inside and onto the elevator. We go back up to the waiting room where Mom has taken over my job of moving the crib. Everyone just kind of gives me sad smiles but nobody comments on my red face.

I sit down and take the crib back, thanking my Mom.

I pull my phone from my pocket and see it lit up with a ton of messages over the last hour, and everyone one of them is from Grace.

Wifey: how is emily

Wifey: is she okay?

Wifey: what are you doing?

Wifey: have you checked her diaper? It's been an hour

Wifey: I want to see you guys.

Wifey: I told you three weeks ago to change your settings so when you flip the switch it vibrates. I bet you're going to do it when you read this lmao

Wifey: babe seriously how is Emmy because my boobs hurt she might be hungry

Wifey: ??

Wifey: can you go to mcdonalds in the morning I really want a sausage egg and cheese mcmuffin

Wifey: okay its been two hours how is emily?

Wifey: daneil

Wifey: daniel*

Wifey: wtf

I hesitate and then I go into my settings and switch it so my phone vibrates on silent.

Me: how are you? You're on your phone. What are they doing to you? Are you okay? I miss you. Does it hurt? I love you

The message goes to read almost immediately.

Wifey: idfk they said I had a hemorrhage or something because one of the nurses didn't connect my IV cord to the damn bag so the meds they were giving me that were supposed to make my uterus contract back to its original side didn't go into me so I started to hemorrhage

Wifey: and I guess they were supposed to massage my uterus? But they didn't do that either

Wifey: its called uterine atony and since my uterus didn't know to contract, my blood vessels started bleeding freely

Wifey: now they're giving me blood and massaging my stomach and it hurts and I'm actually really pissed off. Dr edwards is fucking pissed too though she's screaming at nurses because they didn't do their job. And she said she's going to check emily to make sure shes okay because the nurses are incompetent

Me: how were blood vessels bleeding? I don't understand

Wifey: after I delivered the placenta, the vessels it was attached to were exposed. My uterus needed to contract so the vessels were exposed, but since they didn't give me the meds/massage me, I started bleeding a lot

Me: could it have killed you if I didn't see the blood

Wifey: idk

Me: ask please

Wifey: I don't want to ask

Me: well they kicked me out so you have to ask for me

Wifey: fine

Wifey: dr edwards said that if you didn't notice it until an hour later, I would have probably bled out

One hour. Sixty minutes. Three thousand, six hundred seconds.

If our family didn't come in and Grace and I stayed asleep, my wife would be dead right now.

Me: are you fucking kidding me?

Me: we're transferring hospitals. Fuck this shit

Me: if they don't know how to plug a fucking wire into a bag, they need to be fired. If our family didn't come in tonight, you would be dead right now

Me: we're switching hospitals grace I'm not fucking playing

Wifey: it's really not that big of a deal

Me: yes it is. We're switching hospitals. This is not an argument

The message goes to read and almost a minute later, she replies.

Wifey: fine

Wifey: its not dr edwards fault though

Me: the fuck it's not. She was so ready to run out the damn hospital she didn't check to make sure you were okay. You and our daughter are her fucking patient and she didn't bother to check and make sure you and em were 150% okay

Me: I can't believe this shit. I'm fucking pissed

"Who are you texting so angrily?" Scott asks.

I look up to see everyone looking at me.

"I guess when Grace delivered the placenta, it exposed blood vessels." I say. "And the doctors were supposed to give her some medicine to make her uterus contract back so she wouldn't bleed, but they hooked the bag up and never gave her the damn medicine. They were supposed to massage her uterus and they didn't do that either. Dr. Edwards said if I noticed the blood an hour later, Grace would be dead."

"Oh, you've got to be kidding me." Scott stands up. "That's ridiculous!"

Wifey: this is fucking bullshit they're making me stay until Wednesday

Wifey: motherfucking Wednesday. I'm so mad I'm about to cry

"Now they're making her stay until Wednesday." I say. "Fuck this. I'm finding somebody in charge."

Me: I'm handling it princess I promise

Wifey: send me a picture of Emmy

I look at the baby in the crib and she's sleeping peacefully. I take a picture and send it to Grace, and then I pick up our daughter.

With one hand, I message my wife.

Me: you know they never gave us the fucking ankle thingy either

Wifey: are you serious

Me: yes

Wifey: are you 100% sure It's emily and not some random baby

Me: yes

Wifey: don't let her out of your sight

Me: okay

"I'm going to find somebody in charge." I say.

I sling the diaper bag over my shoulder and carry my baby in her elephant pajamas. I turn on my ringer and shove my phone in my pocket, wandering downstairs to the front desk.

"Is there somebody in charge I can talk to? I want the chief or surgery. I want the highest boss you have."

The woman hesitates, eying my baby.

"I'll get him on the phone."

"Thank you." I say.

I stand back and wait.

My phone chimes and I fish it out of my pocket.

Wifey: don't snitch on edwards ok I like her and she was good to us

Me: she should have stayed

Wifey: well I like her don't tell on her

Me: fine

After a minute, the woman hangs up the phone.

"He's in a surgery." She says.

"Can you please tell him I need to talk to him as soon as possible?"

"Sir, I just spoke with him, and-"

"His nurses almost killed my wife, so please tell him I need to speak with him."

"Right away." She says.

Less than ten minutes later, a man comes off the elevator looking stressed in a white lab coat.

The woman points him in my direction.

"I'm Dr. Lawrence." He sticks his hand out.

"Daniel Grey." I shake his hand with my free hand. "Is there somewhere we can talk?"

"Yes, right this way."

His eyes linger on my baby before he leads me to his office.

He shuts the door.

"Sorry for my lack of clothing. She peed on me." I look down at my daughter and he laughs.

"It's okay. What did you need to talk to me about?"

"Do you have children?" I ask him.

"Yes. Two girls."

I nod.

"My wife just had this one around midnight. She was sleeping but our family came in, so she got up, and blood was gushing down her leg. We were kicked out of the room. My wife texted me and told me that your nurses were supposed to give her medicine for her uterus to contract, but they never connected the IV to the bag. They were supposed to massage her uterus, and they never did that either. My wife's doctor said that if another hour passed with her bleeding undetected, my wife would be dead. Now they're making her stay here until Wednesday, and they've made this a giant hassle. I think you can understand why I'm pissed off right now."

"Let's go up and see what's going on." He says.

"Thank you." I say.

We leave his office and head for the elevator.

"And another thing too, how do I know my daughter was given a proper examination?"

"When we get up there, I will examine her myself. I have been in this job field for thirty years. You can trust me."

"Thank you." I say.

The elevator dings on the floor and you have to go to a lady's desk to get through the doors, but he just walks up and puts his badge up to the machine. We stand back and the doors swing open, and he goes walking down the hall. I follow him with Emily.

"It's this one." I point to Grace's door.

He opens it and goes marching straight into the room.

There is a nurse trying to stick a needle in Grace, and I can see blood my wife is sitting in. She's pale and looks exhausted. Everything is so hectic and I just get more angry. This is bullshit.

"Does somebody want to tell me what's going on here?" He asks loudly. I put my hand on Emily's ear. "Why did this patients husband just come and tell me you almost killed his wife? Why is-" he cuts off, looking at Grace. "What's your name?"

"Gracelyn."

"Why is Gracelyn sitting in blood? How many times have you stuck her with that needle? Why has the proper medication not been admitted? Have you guys given her more blood yet? She's as white as a sheet!"

"We can't find the vain." Dr. Edwards says. "We gave her a uterine massage to get the bleeding to slow."

He washes his hands and puts gloves on, walking over to the nurse. He takes the needle from her hand and very carefully inserts the needle into my wife's arm with one try.

"I want Mrs.-"

"Grey." Gracie says quietly.

"-Mrs. Grey moved to a VIP room, and none of you touch her or their child." He looks at me and Grace. "You guys will pay for nothing but the birth. The hospital stay and all of this is on us." He pauses and looks at the hospital staff. "One of you go get a wheelchair. Do you think you can manage that?" He asks as he tapes the IV down.

"Yes sir." A few of them mutter.

I watch as he connects the blood IV on her other side and connects each tube, one of them to the blood and the other to the medicine, so now she has an IV in both hands. Right before he connects the tube to Grace's IV, he pauses.

"What's your blood type?" He asks

"O-Negative." Grace mumbles. "I'm really tired. Can we please just finish this?"

The doctor looks at the blood bag on the IV, and then he looks at my wife, and then at the nurses.

"O-Negative blood can receive only from O-Negative. This is AB-Positive."

He looks pissed. "I want O-Negative. Now!"

Everyone scatters. The doctor starts to massage Grace's lower stomach again, and she looks uncomfortable.

"I want to go home." She says.

I walk over to her.

"I know baby, I know." I run my fingers through her hair. She reaches up to touch Emily's little foot that's covered by the pajamas.

Her eyes meet mine and I notice how her lips have lost all color. She's pale and she looks scared.

"Am I going to die?" She whispers.

"No." I say right away. "You're going to be fine."

"Because I really don't feel that good." She murmurs.

"Everything is going to be fine. They're going to stop the bleeding."

"What if they can't? Doctor, what's the worst case scenario aside from death?" She asks the chief.

"Worst case scenario is that you get a hysterectomy."

"What is that?" I ask.

"It takes out my uterus." Grace whispers.

"But if you don't have a uterus, we can't have another baby." I say, confused.

"I know."

Dr. Edwards walks back into the room.

"We don't have any O-Negative."

Silence.

Everyone just kind of looks at my wife, and slowly the doctor nods.

"I'll be back."

Without a word, he walks out.

"What happens if I don't get more blood?" Grace asks Dr. Edwards.

She looks down, and I know the answer.

"So take her uterus out." I say.

"We can't."

"Well why not?" I snap.

"Because we can't cut into her. She'll lose more blood."

Oh my god.

"How much time does she have left?" I ask. "If she doesn't get any blood?"

She rubs her forehead and lifts the blanket.

"A half hour. Maybe an hour."

I walk out of the room, rushing down the hall into the waiting room.

"Are any of you O-?" I demand to our family. Everyone looks a little startled.

"I am." Abby says. "Why?"

"They don't have any blood for Grace and she has a half hour before she bleeds out." I plead.

Abby stands up.

"Tell them to nick me."

"Who is this for?" Some guy in the waiting room asks.

"My wife."

He eyes Emily wearily and then stands up.

"I'm O-Negative also. I'll donate for her."

Normally I would be nice and tell him he doesn't have to, but my baby is literally dying right now and I'll take all the help I can get for her.

"Thank you." I say. "Seriously. Thank you so much."

"It's no problem. My sister is having my nephew and she just went into labor. She's going to be a while and I could do some good for the world."

"Alright, follow me." I say.

Abby and the man follow me down the hall again.

I push into Grace's room and she's laying down now and she looks like she's about to fall asleep. Dr. Edwards is connecting her to her medicine and I see her checking the bag multiple times to make sure it's the right thing.

The door shuts behind us and opens a second later, and the chief walks into the room.

"I brought people that are O-Negative."

"Danny, no." Grace mumbles. "I'm not going to sit here and let people bleed for me."

"Well doesn't that suck." Abby says. "Because yes, you actually are."

"No I'm not." She says.

"Sweetheart," I walk over to her and take her hands, which are cold. "If you don't let them do this for you, you are going to die."

Her eyes stay locked with mine for a moment, and then they drift down to our daughter.

"Okay." She whispers finally. "I'll do it."

"Great. Okay." The chief claps his hands. "Who goes first?"

"I'll go first." The guy from the waiting room volunteers. "That way I can be out of here if my sister sends my Mom to find me."

"Abby, can you go get the crib?" I ask.

She walks out and they take the guy to check his blood type for sure. Abby comes back with the crib and I carefully lie Emily down in it.

Grace is shivering and she looks really drowsy and out of it, and I know it's because she's running out of blood.

"I'm cold." She whispers.

I help her sit up and slide my shoes off, slipping into the bed behind her.

She settles back against me and I rub my hands up and down her arms. Abby watches us sadly and then looks down at the floor.

Dr. Edwards goes across the room to check some paper, and Abby crept closer.

"The second she's stable, you need to switch hospitals." She whispers. "And if I were you, I would sue."

Grace rolls to the side and cuddles against me, mumbling about how warm I am.

Abby covers Grace's feet with the blanket, the doctor comes back with the waiting room guy.

They put a needle in his arm and he sits down, and they connect his tube to Grace's IV. The clear tube turns dark red. The doctor checks the bag that Dr. Edwards connected to Grace's IV and nods slightly.

He starts to massage her belly again and I feel her muscles tighten in pain. He checks under the blanket to see how much blood she's losing.

"It looks like it stopped." He says. "I'm going to stay in here, and you let me know if you start feeling tired." He tells the man.

"Okay."

The doctor sits down. I see Emily moving her little hands, and then I hear her make a small noise before she starts screaming.

Abby looks startled.

"Can you get her?" I ask Abby. "Please?"

I don't want to ditch Grace because she stopped shivering. Abby carefully picks Emily up and moves to our side of the bed. Grace shifting slightly and holds her arms out.

"You're really weak." Abby says quietly.

"I'm not going to drop her."

Abby hands Emily to her, and the moment Emily is adjusted in Grace's arms, she stops crying.

She starts to nurse her anyways. I peek over Grace's shoulder so I can see everything from her point of view, and as I get a clear shot of both breasts, I realize she's lucky. She can see boobs all the time.

She looks at the man who is giving his blood to Grace.

"Can we pay you or something to thank you?" She asks.

"That's not necessary." He says.

"What's your name?" Grace asks him.

"Matthew." He responds.

"I'm Grace."

"It's nice to meet you…even in these weird circumstances."

Grace smiles a little and looks down at Emily.

"Danny, if I die, make sure she doesn't let her grades slip." Grace says. "And start a college fund so she can go to a good school. Try to make her love University of Miami, but don't shove it down her throat."

"I don't have to because you're going to be there to do it." I say.

"And make sure you don't leave her in the yard if she doesn't know how to swim yet, especially with the intercoastal right there. She could drown."

"Grace, stop." I say. "I'm not kidding, stop it."

"No. Something could happen, Danny, and you need to know these things."

I bury my head in her shoulder.

"And when she's older and somebody asks for her hand in marriage, girl or guy, make sure it's somebody who loves her for her, and don't say yes unless you're absolutely sure." She pauses. "And also...don't be one of those widows that don't talk about the dead spouse, okay? You can tell her about me." She hesitates. "And no matter what, under any circumstances, she is not allowed alone with my mother." She pauses. "And don't tell her the truth about my past unless she asks why my Mom doesn't come around or something." She's quiet for a minute and I'm hoping she's done, but then she starts talking again. "If another woman comes along and she's good to you and Emily and you get feelings for her, I want you to be with her. You deserve the entire world. You don't need to sit around miserable all the time."

"Grace." I whisper against her skin.

"Yes?"

"Stop it."

I hear her sigh, but she doesn't know how much her words affect me. This isn't something small. This is huge.

"Alright, I'm done anyways." She mutters.

I hesitate, thinking what I've thought since I contractions got bad.

"I'm sorry." I murmur.

"For what?" She asks.

"For saying girls can't handle pain. You're the strongest person I know."

Giving birth with no epidural? She wanted to stop so bad, but she pushed through, literally. She's so strong.

"That was two months ago." She reminds me.

"Well I feel bad for it."

She squeezes my hand with her cold one.

"I love you." She murmurs.

I kiss her neck.

"I love you, too."

*****

Chapter Eighteen: It Won't Be Like This For Long

I hear soft beeping from where they connected Grace's chest to a heart monitor. Her blood pressure is normal and the doctor told me she was stable over three hours ago, but I can't sleep. I tried, but Grace kicked me out of the bed because there isn't enough room for her to sleep comfortably. She's facing me, her eyes shut, her blonde hair thrown behind her. Her lips are slightly parted and I'm watching her breathe.

The chief checked Emily out after Grace fed her, and now Emily is sleeping. I know Emily is going to wake up soon, and I can't wait. If she wakes up, Grace wakes up, and if Grace is awake, she might talk. If Grace talks, I'll be happy again.

We didn't get to bed until five, so it's around eight.

I really want to wake up both of them. Emily so I can hold her and Grace so I can talk to her.

I grab my phone off the couch I'm supposed to sleep on and walk into the bathroom to pee. After the toilet flushing goes quiet again, I wash my hands, dry them, and then use my phone to call the house.

It rings once and then stops.

"Hello?" Scott asks.

I hesitate.

"Did you go to sleep?"

He's quiet for a second, and then, "No, none of us did."

I hesitate, "Why?"

"Did you sleep?" He asks.

"Well...no," I mumble.

"Why not?"

I hesitate, "Probably the same reason you didn't sleep."

"Exactly. We've been sitting by the phone since we got home."

"She's stable." I say. "She's just sleeping, but I'm paranoid."

I hear Emily starting to fuss through the bathroom door so I slip into the hospital room. Grace is starting to stir and Emily's eyes are shut, but she looks like she's about to scream.

Grace peeks her head up to look at me. She rubs her eyes and sighs.

"Who is on the phone?"

"Your Dad." I tell her. She holds her hand out for the phone. I hand it to her.

"Dad?" She asks. "I'm fine. When are you coming back to the hospital?" She pauses. "Well can you go to McDonald's for me? There's twenty bucks in my room at my bedside table." I hear her sigh. "Because I'm hungry. I almost died last night, you know."

"Are you guilting him?" I whisper. She shrugs.

"If it's breakfast time, I want a sausage egg and cheese McMuffin and a caramel frappe with extra caramel drizzle...and make sure they give me-actually, you know what? I want two sausage egg and cheese McMuffins. And I want a hash brown." She pauses again. "No, the mocha one is gross. I want caramel...now, if it's lunch time, I was two McDoubles, a medium fry, a large unsweet tea with lemon...and a crispy snack wrap. Tell them not to put any ranch on it and get honey mustard on the side. I don't know. Get him a Big Mac or something." She looks at me and raises her eyebrows and I nod. "If it's breakfast, get him..."

"Just get the same thing you got for breakfast."

"If it's breakfast get the same thing I got. His drink for lunch is sweet tea with lemon. And you know what? Get Danny a snack wrap too...with no ranch and honey mustard on the side. If there's not enough money..." she trails off. "There should be two twenties in that drawer. You guys can get something too, just make sure they don't put ranch on my snack wrap. Okay. No, I'm fine. Yes. Alright, bye, love you."

She listens for a second and then hangs up.

Emily starts to really cry, so I pick her up.

"I'm standing up." Grace announces.

I hold Emily with one hand and walk over to my wife. She pushes the blankets off of her and I'm relieved to know there isn't any blood on her sheets. She takes my hand and slowly gets out of bed. She stands in front of me for a second.

Her heart monitor speed stayed the same and her blood pressure is the same also.

"How do you feel?"

"I feel like I have to pee." She grabs the IV with the heart monitor connected to it and walks to the bathroom. I follow her with my hand on her arm. I stay with her as she goes to the bathroom and washes her hands, and then I follow her back to the bed.

"I want her." She holds her hands out for Emily.

I give her to her and she lies her down to change her diaper.

"How do you feel now?" I ask.

"I feel tired." She says. "Did you sleep while I slept?"

I hesitate. "No."

She looks at me.

"Well why not?"

"I was worried about you."

"Danny, I'm-"

"Grace, you almost died last night." I cut her off. "There's no reason to not say it. You did. You were telling me what to do with my life and Emily's if you died. You're my wife and my best friend and I love you, but you almost died. I'm allowed to worry."

"You're right." She sighs and looks down at Emily. "It would be messed up if I died and Emily grew up without a Mom, when I had to grow up with a crazy one. Maybe it's just not in the cards for Levinsky girls to have good Mom's."

"Luckily for both of you, you're not Levinsky's. You're Grey's. My Mom is great, Aunt Isabelle is great, and Aunt Marie is great. And you know what? You're great."

"By blood, I'm a Levinsky." She says.

"And by Emily's blood, she's a Grey. Grey's have good Mom's."

"She's a Grey and a Levinsky." She argues.

"Grace." I say softly. "You are a good Mom. While you were pregnant, you made sure to didn't do anything you weren't supposed to. You have been insistent that Emily stay with one of us to protect her. You made them get the thing for her ankle to protect her. You are doing everything you possibly can in this current situation."

She looks down and sighs.

"I just want to take her home."

"I know." I murmur. "Soon."

Grace

On Monday morning, the doctor came in and told Danny and I that Emily was allowed to go home. They discharged her and everything.

But I couldn't leave.

And I told Danny and I had to pee and then I locked myself in the bathroom and cried, because it's not fair.

Why didn't my body know what to do? I could be dead. I could never see Danny again. Never see Emily grow up.

But my husband left me for the first time with Emily alone, and when he came back, he had more clothes.

The doctor came in to check on me and Danny told him that the only way he and Emily are leaving is if I can go with them.

So he stayed.

By Wednesday, I was doing laps around the nursery floor, and Wednesday afternoon I was discharged.

I cried when I got home because I was so happy to be out of there.

My husband, paranoid as ever, called another doctor to check on me and the baby, and she reassured him that both of us were okay.

Now though? It's three in the morning on our first night out of the hospital, and Emily won't stop screaming.

There is no way she's hungry because she already nursed. I tried to feed her again and she wasn't interested. Her temperature is normal, her diaper is clean, her clothes aren't too tight.

I tried a pacifier. I tried cradling her. I tried talking to her, I tried putting her in the swing. In her crib. In the bassinet. In the co sleeper that attaches to our bed. We've tried sharing her, letting other people hold her, but nothing is working. Danny's hair is a wreck and he looks like he's about to scream out of frustration and worry.

And she's woken up the entire house, and we're all in the kitchen and she's cradled against my chest and screaming.

"I don't-I don't know what to do. We've exhausted every obstacle!"

Danny grabs the coffee from the cabinet and a new filter, pulling the machine towards him. He starts a pot and braces his arms against the counter. I can see his muscles clenched in frustration.

During my pregnancy, I would sit and watch videos.

And I've gotten advice from my Aunt's and Danny's Aunt's, and from Beatrice and even doctors and people that have kids.

And the most popular thing I've heard is that sometimes, babies just cry.

I bassinet is in the living room.

I walk over to it and lie her down, and roll it to the kitchen.

"I'm going to let her cry it out."

Everyone looks stressed. My shoulders are tense and I'm exhausted from long nights.

Danny splashes some water on his face and grips the edge of the sink.

There's nothing else to do. There isn't anything she needs.

I stand in front of the bassinet and watch her.

After a few more minutes, her screams lessen until they stop completely. The house falls into silence. The only sound is the dripping of the coffee into the pot. Emily lies there, her eyes wide open, staring at me.

I hear Danny sigh and she looks tense.

I walk over to him and put my hand on his bare back. His skin is smooth and warm.

"Hey." I murmur. He looks at me and he looks exhausted. "Pretty soon she's going to start kindergarten. She's going to spending the night at her friends house. She's going to get her drivers license. She's going to get a boyfriend. She's going to go to college. This right now? The long nights? It's only for a little while. Pretty soon she's going to be gone, living her own life."

He looks past me at the bassinet where Emily is lying and sighs.

"Pretty soon my little girl is going to be in school."

"Exactly. So let's just..." I take a deep breath. "Hang on for now. It's going to be okay."

www.ingramcontent.com/pod-product-compliance
Lightning Source LLC
Chambersburg PA
CBHW072154070526
44585CB00015B/1128